READINGS ON

ANTIGONE

OTHER TITLES IN THE GREENHAVEN PRESS LITERARY COMPANION SERIES:

AMERICAN AUTHORS

Maya Angelou
Stephen Crane
Emily Dickinson
William Faulkner
F. Scott Fitzgerald
Robert Frost
Nathaniel Hawthorne
Ernest Hemingway
Herman Melville
Arthur Miller
Eugene O'Neill
Edgar Allan Poe
John Steinbeck
Mark Twain
Walt Whitman
Thornton Wilder

AMERICAN LITERATURE

The Adventures of
  Huckleberry Finn
The Adventures of Tom
  Sawyer
The Call of the Wild
The Catcher in the Rye
The Crucible
Death of a Salesman
The Glass Menagerie
The Grapes of Wrath
The Great Gatsby
Of Mice and Men
The Old Man and the Sea
The Pearl
The Scarlet Letter
A Separate Peace

BRITISH AUTHORS

Jane Austen
Joseph Conrad
Charles Dickens

BRITISH LITERATURE

Animal Farm
Beowulf
Brave New World
The Canterbury Tales
Great Expectations
Hamlet
Heart of Darkness
Julius Caesar
Lord of the Flies
Macbeth
Pride and Prejudice
Romeo and Juliet
Shakespeare: The Comedies
Shakespeare: The Histories
Shakespeare: The Sonnets
Shakespeare: The Tragedies
A Tale of Two Cities
Wuthering Heights

WORLD AUTHORS

Fyodor Dostoyevsky
Homer
Sophocles

WORLD LITERATURE

All Quiet on the Western
  Front
The Diary of a Young Girl
A Doll's House

THE GREENHAVEN PRESS
Literary Companion
TO WORLD LITERATURE

READINGS ON

ANTIGONE

Don Nardo, *Book Editor*

David L. Bender, *Publisher*
Bruno Leone, *Executive Editor*
Bonnie Szumski, *Series Editor*

Greenhaven Press, San Diego, CA

Every effort has been made to trace the owners of copyrighted material. The articles in this volume may have been edited for content, length, and/or reading level. The titles have been changed to enhance the editorial purpose. Those interested in locating the original source will find the complete citation on the first page of each article.

Library of Congress Cataloging-in-Publication Data

Readings on Antigone / Don Nardo, book editor.
     p.   cm. — (The Greenhaven Press literary
companion to world literature)
  Includes bibliographical references and index.
  ISBN 1-56510-968-6 (pbk. : alk. paper). —
ISBN 1-56510-969-4 (lib. : alk. paper)
  1. Sophocles. Antigone. 2. Antigone (Greek mythology)
in literature. I. Nardo, Don, 1947– . II. Series.
PA4413.A7R44   1999
882'.01—dc21
                           98-51924
                               CIP

Cover photo: Stock Montage, Inc.

Copyright ©1999 by Greenhaven Press, Inc.
PO Box 289009
San Diego, CA 92198-9009
Printed in the U.S.A.

66Wisdom is by far the
greatest part of joy,
and reverence toward the
gods must be safeguarded.
The mighty words of the
proud are paid in full
with mighty blows of fate,
and at long last
those blows will teach us
wisdom.99

—Sophocles, *Antigone*
(Robert Fagles' translation)

CONTENTS

Chapter 1: The Plot, Themes, and Ideas of *Antigone*

decent burial is seen as stronger than Creon's, which puts the good of community above family considerations. Yet some scholars advocate that their positions are equally valid. One must inevitably prevail and the other's loss is tragic.

Chapter 2: Antigone's Qualities and Motivations

Chapter 3: The Play's Other Characters

Foreword

> *"'Tis the good reader that
> makes the good book."*
>
> Ralph Waldo Emerson

The story's bare facts are simple: The captain, an old and scarred seafarer, walks with a peg leg made of whale ivory. He relentlessly drives his crew to hunt the world's oceans for the great white whale that crippled him. After a long search, the ship encounters the whale and a fierce battle ensues. Finally the captain drives his harpoon into the whale, but the harpoon line catches the captain about the neck and drags him to his death.

A simple story, a straightforward plot—yet, since the 1851 publication of Herman Melville's *Moby-Dick*, readers and critics have found many meanings in the struggle between Captain Ahab and the whale. To some, the novel is a cautionary tale that depicts how Ahab's obsession with revenge leads to his insanity and death. Others believe that the whale represents the unknowable secrets of the universe and that Ahab is a tragic hero who dares to challenge fate by attempting to discover this knowledge. Perhaps Melville intended Ahab as a criticism of Americans' tendency to become involved in well-intentioned but irrational causes. Or did Melville model Ahab after himself, letting his fictional character express his anger at what he perceived as a cruel and distant god?

Although literary critics disagree over the meaning of *Moby-Dick*, readers do not need to choose one particular interpretation in order to gain an understanding of Melville's novel. Instead, by examining various analyses, they can gain numerous insights into the issues that lie under the surface of the basic plot. Studying the writings of literary critics can also aid readers in making their own assessments of *Moby-Dick* and other literary works and in developing analytical thinking skills.

The Greenhaven Literary Companion Series was created with these goals in mind. Designed for young adults, this unique anthology series provides an engaging and comprehensive introduction to literary analysis and criticism. The essays included in the Literary Companion Series are chosen for their accessibility to a young adult audience and are expertly edited in consideration of both the reading and comprehension levels of this audience. In addition, each essay is introduced by a concise summation that presents the contributing writer's main themes and insights. Every anthology in the Literary Companion Series contains a varied selection of critical essays that cover a wide time span and express diverse views. Wherever possible, primary sources are represented through excerpts from authors' notebooks, letters, and journals and through contemporary criticism.

Each title in the Literary Companion Series pays careful consideration to the historical context of the particular author or literary work. In-depth biographies and detailed chronologies reveal important aspects of authors' lives and emphasize the historical events and social milieu that influenced their writings. To facilitate further research, every anthology includes primary and secondary source bibliographies of articles and/or books selected for their suitability for young adults. These engaging features make the Greenhaven Literary Companion Series ideal for introducing students to literary analysis in the classroom or as a library resource for young adults researching the world's great authors and literature.

Exceptional in its focus on young adults, the Greenhaven Literary Companion Series strives to present literary criticism in a compelling and accessible format. Every title in the series is intended to spark readers' interest in leading American and world authors, to help them broaden their understanding of literature, and to encourage them to formulate their own analyses of the literary works that they read. It is the editors' hope that young adult readers will find these anthologies to be true companions in their study of literature.

INTRODUCTION

Of Sophocles' many plays, *Antigone* was one of the most popular and often-performed in antiquity. Indeed, according to tradition its introduction in Sophocles' native Athens shortly before 441 B.C. was so successful it helped to get him elected as one of the city's ten generals. The play's central theme, the conflict over whether the burial of a corpse should be allowed, was popular with ancient audiences. In ancient Greece, after all, proper burial was seen as a divine ordinance, a ceremony demanded by the gods. The view may have been based on the then-common belief that the unburied dead were forbidden from entering the underworld and had to roam the earth forever.

Yet if this question of proper burial had been the only issue in the play, it is unlikely that *Antigone* would have captured the imaginations of ancient audiences to the extent it did. Nor, certainly, would it be revived, performed, read, and studied so often today. There is, in fact, much more to the play than that single issue, which explains why both ancients and moderns have found it so compelling. As the noted classical scholar C.M. Bowra points out:

> The *Antigone* cannot have owed its first success to any ephemeral [momentary] or topical attractiveness in its subject. It deals with a theme [the burial issue] that in its narrowest aspects means little to us, but it raises broader issues which still have such vitality that it has been claimed to deal with matters so universal as the conflict of family and state, of individual and government, of human and divine laws.[1]

Each succeeding human generation has witnessed its share of families or individuals who have resisted or challenged state authority. And arguments over whether human-made rules should take precedence over god-given ones have echoed through the ages and continue today.

It is precisely because these themes still resonate in human societies that numerous modern playwrights have written their own treatments of Sophocles' *Antigone*. Updated versions by France's Jean Anouilh, Germany's Bertolt Brecht, and others place the characters in modern settings, such as Nazi Germany. But they develop, with varying degrees of success, many of the same themes the ancient version does: the consequences of war and political strife, love of and loyalty to family, loyalty to and support for the community, the right of an individual to challenge the state, and reverence for God. The exploration of these and other universal aspects of the human condition is what makes Antigone's story as fresh and relevant today as it was when Sophocles first presented it.

The essays selected for the Greenhaven Literary Companion to Sophocles' *Antigone* provide teachers and students with a wide range of information and opinion about the play and its author's style, themes, and outlook on the human condition. All of the authors of the essays are or were (until their deaths) professors at leading colleges and universities, noted scholars specializing in ancient Greek literature and drama, or widely respected authorities on Sophocles and his works.

Among this companion volume's several special features are that each of the essays explains or discusses in detail a specific, narrowly focused topic; the introduction to each essay previews the main points; and inserts interspersed within the essays serve as examples of ideas expressed by the authors, offer supplementary information, and/or add authenticity and color. These inserts come from *Antigone,* from plays and other works by Sophocles' ancient contemporaries, including the playwright Aeschylus and historian Herodotus, or from modern scholarly descriptions of ancient Greek theater, religion, and society.

Above all, this companion book is designed to enhance the reader's understanding and enjoyment of a timeless, classic tale of love, anger, courage, stubbornness, defiance, punishment, and self-sacrifice. Indeed, *Antigone* is alive with the interplay of human emotions. In the words of the late great modern scholar H.D.F. Kitto, it is "a passionate story of conflict and suffering, presented as directly and as vividly as any such story has ever been."[2]

NOTES

1. *Sophoclean Tragedy.* Oxford: Clarendon Press, 1944, p. 63.
2. *Form and Meaning in Drama: A Study of Six Greek Plays and of Hamlet.* London: Methuen, 1956, p. 176.

SOPHOCLES AND *ANTIGONE*

The course of the action in *Antigone,* one of the greatest plays ever written, has reached a dramatic turning point. A young boy leads the blind seer Teiresias onto the stage to confront Creon, who has been king of Thebes for only a day. And what an eventful, nerve-wracking day it has been for Creon. The day before, Eteocles, son of the former Theban king Oedipus, had been king. Another of Oedipus's sons, Polynices, had led an army against the city, intent on unseating his brother, but the attack had failed and both brothers were killed in the fighting. Creon claimed the right, as their uncle, to take the throne. His first official act had been to label Polynices a traitor and deny him a traditional burial, adding that anyone who did attempt to bury him would receive a death sentence:

> Eteocles, who died fighting for Thebes, excelling in all arms: he shall be buried, crowned with a hero's honors. . . . But as for his blood brother, Polynices . . . who thirsted to drink his kinsmen's blood and sell the rest to slavery . . . a proclamation has forbidden the city to dignify him with burial, [or] mourn him at all. No, he must be left unburied, his corpse carrion for the birds and dogs to tear, an obscenity for the citizens to behold!¹

Undaunted by this harsh decree, Oedipus's daughter Antigone performed her brother's burial rites. And true to his warning, Creon condemned the young girl to be executed.

Now, only moments after guards led Antigone away to her doom, Teiresias has appeared. The old prophet tells the king that omens and other signs indicate that the gods are angry about the decree forbidding Polynices' burial. Teiresias warns that Creon must rescind the decree or face the loss of his own son to the terrible forces of divine retribution:

> The chariot of the sun will not race through so many circuits more, before you have surrendered one born of your own loins, your own flesh and blood, a corpse for corpses given in return, since you have . . . robbed the gods below the earth,

keeping a dead body here in the bright air, unburied, unsung, unhallowed by the [traditional burial] rites.[2]

What makes this scene pivotal is that Creon still has time to lift the decree and save Antigone from her untimely demise. He has no way of knowing it, of course, but by saving her he would also save his own son, Haemon, who, anguished over Antigone's death, will commit suicide, as well as Creon's wife, Eurydice, who, on hearing of Haemon's death, will take her own life. But the arrogant Creon does not heed Teiresias's warning in time. And all three of these deaths occur in rapid succession.

The scene between Creon and Teiresias is also important because Sophocles introduces the gods into a story that has so far only involved human characters. The gods do not appear on the stage in person. Yet their powerful will and presence are felt through Teiresias's words, as well as through the tragic series of deaths that follow. It is Creon's failure to heed their wisdom in time that allows the tragedy's final events to unfold. Thus, as the noted scholar C.M. Bowra says:

> *Antigone* is a tragedy of human folly. The folly is of a special kind, a blindness of soul which makes a man in high position do what is wrong. With his illusions the play is much concerned, and indeed its conflict takes place at a level where the illusions of men resist and rebut the claims of reality and truth.[3]

Another critical element of the scene is the playwright's perceptive and ironic observation that the gods' wisdom, and perhaps any and all wisdom, may be imparted through unlikely sources. Teiresias is blind, yet he sees truths that sighted people, including Creon, cannot. Also, a boy guides the seer onto the stage. The ancient Greeks saw innocent children as possessing special insights about life that adults often overlooked. And finally, it was Antigone who had insisted all along that burying her brother was the right thing to do. In Greece's strongly male-dominated society, a woman teaching a man, especially a ruler, the correct ethical course was a highly unexpected and unusual event.

This brief analysis of a single scene from *Antigone* reveals just a few of the play's insights into the human condition and the relationship between human actions and divine will and judgment. The confrontation between Creon and Antigone, for instance, explores political concepts, among them a ruler's responsibility to protect the community and an individual's right to challenge the state. It also raises questions about which laws are paramount and most binding—human or divine ones? In addition, Antigone's determination to give her brother a proper burial no matter what the consequences exemplifies the power of love and the importance of loyalty to family. These and other universal themes developed with consummate skill in the play make it one of the most riveting and important works in Western literature. Indeed, even if *Antigone* had been Sophocles' only work, it would have been enough to earn him a firm place in history's pantheon of great writers.

THE SOURCES FOR SOPHOCLES' LIFE

Antigone was not Sophocles' only play, of course, which has proved most fortunate for the generations that succeeded him. He wrote 123 plays in all, seven of which have survived the ravages of time—*Ajax* (written about 447 B.C.), *Antigone* (ca. 441), *Oedipus the King* (ca. 429), *The Women of Trachis* (ca. 428), *Electra* (ca. 415), *Philoctetes* (409), and *Oedipus at Colonus* (406). Each of these works is a masterpiece in its own right. And many literary critics and scholars consider *Oedipus the King* (also *Oedipus Rex* or *Oedipus Tyrannus*) to be the greatest tragedy ever written. It was from this morbid but compelling tale of a man who unknowingly murders his father and then marries his mother that the modern psychoanalyst Sigmund Freud derived his idea for the "Oedipus complex," which profoundly influenced the theory and practice of psychiatry in the twentieth century.

The loss of Sophocles' other 116 plays is itself a great tragedy. Considering the tremendous literary and intellectual influence of the surviving seven, one cannot help but wonder how much greater his impact might have been had all or at least most of his works survived. Another slice of misfortune is that few ancient documents recording the details of Sophocles' personal life and career have survived. Most were written long after his death and offer little information.

Of the two more substantial sources about the playwright, the most informative and valuable is an anonymous biography titled *Sophocles' Life and Works,* usually referred to simply as the *Life.* It was discovered in a thirteenth-century collection of his plays and its date is unknown. Another, much shorter version of the playwright's life is found in the *Suidas* (or *Suidas Lexicon*), a tenth-century Greek encyclopedia. It offers a few facts not found in the *Life* and also differs from the latter on certain details, such as the number of prizes the dramatist won.

According to these sources, Sophocles was born in 497 or 496 B.C. in Colonus, then a village situated about a mile north of Athens's famous central hill, the Acropolis. At that time, Attica, the peninsula of eastern Greece dominated and controlled by Athens, was divided into many such villages, called demes. The future playwright's father, Sophillus, perhaps a weapons-maker, was evidently wealthy and one of their deme's leading citizens.

Coming from a rich family, it is certain that Sophocles was well educated. Young, upper-class Athenian boys received excellent, well-rounded educations, partly because they were expected eventually to assume leading roles in local government. The tasks of debating and voting on laws in Athens's democratic assembly, of leading the army, of conducting foreign policy, and of overseeing the arts, which were largely community- and state-supported, demanded that such leaders be highly informed and versatile individuals.

A THEATRICAL INNOVATOR

Sophocles likely gained some of his early training from the city's several religious festivals, in which a large proportion of the population often took part. Each year, for instance, between one and two thousand Athenian boys sang in the choruses that performed at these festivals, which included the grand City Dionysia dramatic festival, held at the end of March. For five or six days, playwrights presented their works, the best (or at least the most popular) of which won prizes. Because positions in the choruses usually rotated among the citizens, most, if not all, Athenian boys sooner or later took part. It is probable, therefore, that Sophocles was bitten by the acting bug, so to speak, during this youthful firsthand contact with music and theater.

Some evidence also suggests that Sophocles studied drama under Aeschylus, the world's first great playwright and by far the most dominant figure in Greek theater in the first decades of the fifth century B.C. It is tempting to picture Sophocles as an aspiring dramatist, still rough around the edges and learning his craft by acting in the choruses of some of Aeschylus's early plays. At the very least, Sophocles must have attended performances of all or most of Aeschylus's plays.

As he matured, Sophocles proved himself to be a great dramatist in his own right. He competed often with Aeschylus in the great Dionysia and became an important theatrical innovator. Aeschylus had earlier introduced the device of a second actor. Playwrights had initially limited themselves to telling fairly simple stories with two or three characters, which a lone actor portrayed by repeatedly changing masks (a stage convention at the time; there was a different mask for each general character type). Adding a second actor greatly expanded the scope of the stories writers could present because it allowed them to depict twice as many characters. The potential of this innovation was not lost on Sophocles, who eventually introduced a third actor. With three actors alternating characters, a dramatist could show more characters and therefore tell a more complex story. Sophocles may also have carried this idea a step further near the end of his career by utilizing a fourth actor.

Indeed, Sophocles typically stressed character development, often focusing on his leading characters' mix of personal traits and motivations—both good and bad, strong and weak—that influenced their struggles to deal with profound ethical dilemmas. In keeping with this approach, he frequently treated the fifteen-member chorus as a character in its own right. The renowned fourth-century-B.C. Greek philosopher Aristotle praised Sophocles for having the chorus participate directly in the action of the story rather than stay primarily in the background.[4] In *Antigone,* for example, the chorus represents a group of Theban elders. They witness the action and provide important commentary and judgments about Creon's decree and Antigone's defiance.

Evidence suggests that Sophocles also introduced the tetralogy, a group of four plays written and produced by the same dramatist. Three were tragedies having unrelated subjects and the fourth was a "satyr play," a shorter, comic, and often obscene takeoff on a well-known myth or other popular tale.[5] The purpose of the satyr play was to provide the audience with some measure of relief from the emotionally draining tragedies. After Sophocles began using it, this combination of plays became the most common. The five- to six-day Dionysia festival would therefore feature a tetralogy by each of three playwrights—twelve plays in all.

The *Life* and other ancient sources also attribute other innovations to Sophocles, including costumes, painted scenery, and props for the actors. The truth of these claims remains uncertain. What *is* certain is that Sophocles was much more than a mere playwright. He was most often the play's producer, director, stage manager, and probably a chorus member or extra as well.

A MODEL FOR THE IDEAL CITIZEN

It is uncertain when Sophocles wrote and produced his first theatrical work. Modern scholars are fairly sure, however, that he won his first victory in the City Dionysia in 468 B.C., when he was about twenty-eight, for a play titled *Triptolemus.* According to the first-century-A.D. Greek biographer and moralist Plutarch, the play's premiere was controversial because of an intense rivalry between Sophocles' supporters and those of the then-reigning master, Aeschylus. The archon (administrator) of the dramatic contests broke with tradition and called on Cimon, a popular politician and general, to pick a winner. "When Sophocles, who was still a young man, presented his first trilogy," Plutarch writes,

> Apsephion the archon noticed that the spirit of rivalry and partisanship was running high among the audience and decided not to appoint the judges of the contest by lot [random drawing], as was usually done. Instead, when Cimon and his fellow-generals entered the theater and made the usual libation [sacrificial offering of wine or other liquids] to the god Dionysus, he did not allow them to leave, but obliged them to take the oath and sit as judges.... In consequence, the fact that the judges were so distinguished raised the whole contest to a far more ambitious level. Sophocles won the prize, and it is said that Aeschylus was so distressed and indignant that he ... [retired] in anger to Sicily.[6]

Sophocles continued to distinguish himself as a versatile writer-producer-director in the Athenian dramatic festivals for six more decades. Play production did not occupy all of his time, however, for he periodically served his native Athens in various responsible and sometimes important public offices. In 443 B.C., Pericles, the city's most popular and powerful politician at the time, appointed him chief treasurer in charge of collecting money from the member states of the far-flung Athenian empire.

The dramatist achieved an even more powerful post three years later when he was elected one of Athens's ten *strategoi,* the military generals who commanded the armies and carried out state foreign policy. There may or may not be any truth to the later story that he won the election because of the popularity of *Antigone,* produced one or two years before. What is certain is that he managed to juggle frequent and deep involvement in public affairs with a successful professional career. This made him a visible and undoubtedly highly respected model of the ideal democratic citizen that Pericles described in his famous funeral oration:

> Our public men have, besides politics, their private affairs to attend to, and our ordinary citizens, though occupied with the pursuits of industry, are still fair judges of public matters; for, unlike any other nation, we regard the citizen who takes no part in these duties not as unambitious but as useless. . . . I doubt if the world can produce a man . . . equal to so many emergencies, and graced by so happy a versatility as the Athenian.[7]

A GENTLEMAN ALWAYS

Though some information about Sophocles' generalship and other tidbits of his public life have survived, little is known about his private life and personal character. His colleague, the famous comic playwright Aristophanes, provided a clue in his play *Frogs,* produced shortly after Sophocles death. The gods Dionysus and Heracles, portrayed comically in the play, discuss Dionysus's desire to bring the playwright Euripides back from the dead. "Why resurrect Euripides instead of Sophocles?" Heracles asks. Dionysus answers, "Euripides, the clever rogue, would aid my kidnap scheme; while Sophocles, gentleman always, is a gentleman still."[8] Since Aristophanes knew Sophocles personally, we can be fairly certain of the accuracy of this description.

Regarding Sophocles' family relationships, he was married at least once. His wife, Nicostrate, bore him a son, Iophon, who himself became a tragic poet. The *Suidas* mentions several other sons about whom nothing is known. Sophocles also had a grandson, himself named Sophocles, who wrote some forty plays and won several dramatic competitions, and in the third century B.C. another of his descendants bearing his name wrote at least fifteen tragedies.

Sophocles himself died in 406 B.C., shortly after presenting his last play, *Oedipus at Colonus.* Though written more than thirty years after *Antigone,* its story takes place before Polynices' attack on Thebes, the act that precipitates the tragic events of the earlier play. The cause of the playwright's death, though much speculated about by later scholars, remains unknown; however considering his advanced age, about ninety, natural causes seems most likely. The tradition that he passed away while reciting odes from *Antigone* to his friends is charming but unconfirmed.

The dramatist left behind an enormous literary legacy and a popular following. The proof is his extraordinary record of victories in the dramatic contests, which no other playwright in the long history of the Greek festivals ever matched. Ancient sources all agree that he won the great Dionysia competition at least eighteen times, and no less than six other victories are recorded for other contests. Moreover, states the *Life,* although the judges often awarded him second place, he never once came in third.

ANTIGONE'S EARLY HISTORY

It is unknown what prize, if any, *Antigone* won when Sophocles first presented it. In fact, modern scholars have uncovered very few solid facts about the play's early history. Because no yearly lists of fifth-century-B.C. Athenian play production have survived, dating its composition and first presentation is a matter of educated guesswork; the period of 442–441 B.C., shortly before the playwright's election as *strategos,* seems most likely. There is no way to know when and how often the play was revived in succeeding years. But it must have been fairly often. In the following century Aristotle quoted from it repeatedly in his *Politics,* and the great Athenian orator Demosthenes cited one of Creon's speeches to make a point in a court case; both men apparently took it for granted that their audiences were quite familiar with the work.

But though frequent performances enhanced *Antigone*'s reputation, they also threatened the integrity of the original text. Noted scholar Bernard Knox points out:

> Quite apart from the compounded errors and deliberate omissions ... which might occur in the book text, there was undoubtedly much distortion in the versions staged by the traveling theatrical companies which, in the fourth century [B.C.], took the classics of Attic drama to every corner of the Greek world. Theatrical producers, as we know from the bizarre versions of Shakespeare's plays performed in the seventeenth and eighteenth centuries, have no qualms when it comes to cutting or adding to suit the fashion of the time.[9]

In an effort to discourage such textual distortions, in 330 B.C. an Athenian statesman named Lycurgus established official texts of *Antigone* and other great fifth-century plays. Producers, at least in Athens, had to follow these texts. Almost a century later, Greek scholars working in Alexandria, Egypt, produced carefully edited versions of the plays, recapturing the original texts as best as they could. Modern texts of *Antigone* derive from the version made in Alexandria in this period.

In the next six centuries, when Rome ruled Greece, the plays of Sophocles and his Athenian colleagues were performed increasingly less frequently. Eventually, no more copies were made and existing ones began to deteriorate and crumble. The exception consisted of a small selection of plays by each of the masters, probably copied and maintained for scholarly and school use. This is how seven of Sophocles' plays, including *Antigone,* managed to survive the end of antiquity, roughly coinciding with the collapse of the Roman Empire in the fifth and sixth centuries A.D. In the Byzantine capital of Constantinople, scholars continued to copy the texts for school use for several more centuries.[10] Then, during the Renaissance, which began in the late 1300s, Europeans rediscovered their Greek heritage, and demand for manuscripts of the classic texts sharply increased. Copies of *Antigone* remained handwritten, as they had always been, until the first printed version of the play appeared in 1502.

RIGHT VERSUS WRONG OR RIGHT VERSUS RIGHT?

Since that time, many stage productions of *Antigone* have been mounted in various countries and in various languages. The first professional production in the United States opened on April 7, 1845, at the Palmo Opera House in New York City. Some noted recent professional American productions were those at New York's Lincoln Center in May 1971 and at San Francisco's American Conservatory Theater in February 1993.[11] *Antigone* has proved most popular, however, on college stages. At least seventy-five productions of the play were presented by American college theater groups between 1882 and 1936 alone. In addition, a film version of *Antigone* appeared in 1961.

Meanwhile, from early modern times to the present, numerous scholars have studied the play and discussed and debated its themes, character motivations, and social, political, and moral implications. Perhaps the most debated question of all has been: Who is right, Antigone or Creon? Is Antigone morally justified in choosing loyalty to family over the needs and laws of the community? Or is Creon's position, that the good of the community should take precedence over personal concerns, the correct one? One of the most important of the play's early commentators, German philosopher Georg W.F. Hegel (1770–1831), did not take sides on the issue. In his highly influential interpretation, the conflict is not between a right side and wrong side but between what are essentially two right sides. Antigone and Creon argue and act from more or less equally justifiable positions, says Hegel; the fact that these positions cannot be reconciled is the source of the tragedy.[12]

Many later scholars have variously agreed or disagreed with Hegel's interpretations. A majority have sided to one degree or another with Antigone, maintaining that Sophocles himself viewed her stand as having more moral force than Creon's. They usually cite the play's last lines, spoken by the Chorus, which seem to state its overriding lesson:

> Wisdom is by far the greatest part of joy,
> and reverence toward the gods must be safeguarded.
> The mighty words of the proud are paid in full
> with mighty blows of fate, and at long last
> those blows will teach us wisdom.[13]

The meaning of these lines appears plain. The "proud" one whose "mighty words" fate punishes with "mighty blows" is Creon, who, in refusing Polynices' burial, shows the gods irreverence and pays a terrible price for it. That price, the loss of his wife and son, teaches him the "wisdom" he earlier lacked. Sophocles' placement of this powerful statement at the end of the drama does strongly suggest that his sympathies rested more with Antigone than with Creon. As Bowra puts it:

> We may be sure that the Chorus speaks for the poet. It is as silent about Antigone as it is emphatic about Creon. There is no hint that she has in any way acted wrongly or that her death should be regarded as a righteous punishment.[14]

THE LIGHT OF UNDERSTANDING

Still, it is clear from the content of some of Creon's speeches, as well as from the fact that Creon has a good deal more stage time than Antigone, that the playwright by no means meant to discount Creon's position. And many scholars, even if they ultimately side with Antigone, admit that Creon has some admirable qualities and motives. Whatever his later mistakes, argues classical scholar D.W. Lucas, Creon begins with "an excess of virtue" and should not be seen as an ignoble character:

> The manifesto which is the prelude to his decree that the traitor shall not be buried would be acceptable to the wisest and most benevolent of kings. He intends to rule without fear or favor, putting the interest of the city first in all things. Never will the enemy of the city be a friend to him, because it is on the prosperity and welfare of the city that all else depends, and without it we can have no friends.[15]

In a very real way, then, even if Creon's decree and condemnation of Antigone are morally wrong, his mistakes and the punishment he subsequently suffers for them make him as much a tragic figure as she. The idea that the play has two central tragic figures, which many experts accept, is ably summarized here by noted scholar David Seale:

> The focus in the final scenes of the play is on Creon. This is not to diminish the significance of Antigone. But the play does not *belong* to her, just as it does not belong to Creon. It is their relationship which is tragic. . . . Antigone's death is prerequisite to Creon's recognition [of his mistakes]. And his recognition is achieved through the sight of his [dead] dear ones. Only in this way does Creon understand the ties of family for which Antigone was willing to die. The play begins with Antigone's family and ends with Creon's. The importance of the two figures also means that the composite picture of the single tragic hero is broken down and the qualities which typically make up the heroic mold in a Sophoclean play are in a sense shared between two main figures. Thus Creon is not dignified, as Antigone certainly is, by a heroic refusal to yield, while Antigone does not suffer from the blindness which afflicts Creon.[16]

Indeed, as Sophocles and his colleagues recognized so well, blindness to life's underlying truths and realities often makes people act rashly and destructively and thereby causes much unnecessary pain and misery. Creon learned this lesson too late. But through the situations and lines of this immortal play, Sophocles offers each new generation the chance to benefit from that character's mistakes. And in the process, hopefully, the light of understanding helps, in some small measure, to improve the human condition. "Life has its own unbreakable laws," remarks H.D.F. Kitto, a noted expert on Greek tragedy,

> and in it, only half-hidden, are terrible forces. These we must always respect. The saving virtue is "understanding," with reverence towards the gods, which implies reverence toward the ultimate claims of humanity.[17]

NOTES

1. Sophocles, *Antigone* 218–231, in Robert Fagles, trans., *Sophocles: The Three Theban Plays:* Antigone, Oedipus the King, Oedipus at Colonus. New York: Penguin Books, 1984, p. 68.

2. *Antigone* 1182–1190, in Fagles' translation, p. 115.

3. *Sophoclean Tragedy.* Oxford: Clarendon Press, 1944, p. 114.

4. See *Poetics* 18.25; many translations available.

5. Satyrs were mythical creatures, usually pictured as half-man and half-goat. They were originally associated with the fertility god Dionysus, whom Athens's City Dionysia dramatic festival honored. The chorus members in these bawdy plays dressed as satyrs. The only satyr play that has survived complete is the *Cyclops* (ca. 410 B.C.), by Sophocles' younger colleague Euripides.

6. *Life of Cimon* 8, in Ian Scott-Kilvert, trans., *The Rise and Fall of Athens: Nine Greek Lives by Plutarch.* New York: Penguin Books, 1960, p. 150. Plutarch's use of the term *trilogy*, meaning a group of three plays usually related by theme, instead of the term *tetralogy*, is probably an error.

7. Quoted in Thucydides, *The Peloponnesian War* 2.40–2.41, published as *The Landmark Thucydides: A Comprehensive Guide to the Peloponnesian War.* Trans. Richard Crawley, ed. Robert B. Strassler. New York: Simon and Schuster, 1996, pp. 113–14.

8. Translated by R.H. Webb, in Moses Hadas, ed., *The Complete Plays of Aristophanes.* New York: Bantam Books, 1962, p. 371.

9. "A Note on the Text of Sophocles," in Fagles' translation, p. 390.

10. The remains of the eastern sector of the Roman Empire, the Byzantine Empire, survived until 1453, when the Ottoman Turks sacked Constantinople.

11. For details and reviews of these productions, see Karelisa V. Hartigan, *Greek Tragedy on the American Stage: Ancient Drama in the Commercial Theater, 1882–1994.* Westport, CT: Greenwood Press, 1995, pp. 11–12, 112–18.

12. Some later scholars have suggested that this summary of Hegel's views on the play is oversimplified and in any case misleading. C.M. Bowra, for example, cautioned, "Hegel used the *Antigone* to illustrate his view of tragedy . . . and existence. He drew his own conclusions . . . as he was fully entitled to do. But his views are not those of Sophocles," who himself *did not* "maintain that Creon and Antigone were equally right in the eyes of their creator." (*Sophoclean Tragedy*, p. 66)

13. *Antigone* 1466–1470, Fagles' translation, p. 128.

14. *Sophoclean Tragedy*, p. 66.

15. *The Greek Tragic Poets.* New York: W.W. Norton, 1959, p. 141.

16. *Vision and Stagecraft in Sophocles.* Chicago: University of Chicago Press, 1982, p. 107.

17. *Form and Meaning in Drama: A Study of Six Greek Plays and of* Hamlet. London: Methuen, 1956, pp. 177–78.

THE THEBAN SAGA OF MYTHS

The story told in Sophocles' *Antigone* was based in large part on myths that were already ancient to the classical Greeks, that is, the Greeks who lived in Sophocles' era (the fifth and fourth centuries B.C.). Some Greek myths consisted of single tales, each of which might depict some well-known hero's exploit, the death of ill-fated lovers, or the wrath of an angry god. Other myths were part of larger collections of tales, called cycles or sagas. The usual myth cycle dealt with the history and fate of a city or kingdom and the noble families who ruled it, and explored both the best and worst aspects of the human condition and spirit. Typical themes included ambition, greed, arrogance, war, heroism (and cowardice), murder, revenge, loyalty to family or community (or betrayal of one or both), divine intervention (including both punishment and forgiveness of mortals), and personal redemption or rebirth. Perhaps the most famous example is the Trojan myth cycle, describing the fall of Troy (an important trading city in northwestern Asia Minor, what is now Turkey) at the hands of a group of Greek kings.[1]

Another popular group of myths in classical times—the one which contains Antigone's story—was the Theban saga, which tells the sweeping story of the founding of the city of Thebes and the exploits and problems of its early rulers. In ancient times, Thebes was the leading city of Boeotia (pronounced bee-OH-shya), the region of the Greek mainland lying just north of the Athenian territory of Attica. The city rose on a low ridge overlooking central Boeotia's two small lowland plains. And Thebes's acropolis (central hill, usually used as a fortress) was called the Cadmea, after the city's founder, Cadmus.

By the sixth century B.C., the saga of Cadmus and his descendants, summarized below, had been collected into three epic poems—the *Oedipodia*, *Thebaïd*, and *Epigoni*. Unfortunately, these works are lost. However, most of their contents

26

are known from descriptions or adaptations by various ancient writers. The Theban myths were extremely popular with the great fifth-century-B.C. Athenian dramatists, for instance. In addition to Sophocles, who explored them in his *Oedipus the King, Oedipus at Colonus,* and *Antigone,* Aeschylus used them as the basis for his *Seven Against Thebes* and Euripides for *The Phoenician Women* and *The Bacchae.*[2] Because Greek playgoers were so familiar with the stories behind these works, a playwright did not need to identify or explain his references to people and situations that appeared in the saga before or after the events depicted in his play.

THE FOUNDING OF A GREAT CITY

The Theban saga began long ago, in the legendary, colorful, and heroic age when the gods frequently descended to earth and interacted with humans. One day, Zeus, leader of the gods, caught sight of a beautiful young woman walking on the Mediterranean's eastern shore. She was Europa, daughter of the king of the Phoenician city of Tyre. The god was so taken with her that he disguised himself as a bull and enticed her to climb onto his back. As soon as she did so, he bore her, swimming with powerful strokes, across the sea to the large Greek island of Crete.

Back in Tyre, Europa's father, King Agenor, was distraught over her disappearance. He ordered his son, Cadmus, to go looking for her. Realizing that the world was so vast that it might take forever to find his sister, Cadmus decided to ask the oracle at Delphi, in central Greece, for help in locating her. The oracle was a priestess who heard and answered questions posed to her by religious and other kinds of pilgrims.[3] Her pronouncements were believed to come directly from Apollo, the god to whom the Delphic shrine was dedicated. When Cadmus, who was accompanied by a few close companions, asked where to look for Europa, the oracle told him that he need no longer search for her. Instead, he should pursue his own destiny, which promised to be unique and lead to momentous events. "You will encounter a young cow," the oracle told him. "Follow it until it lays down to rest. On that spot you should establish a new city."

Sure enough, Cadmus came upon the cow, and he obediently followed it as it meandered from place to place. In time, it led him across some rugged mountains, into the land of Boeotia, and finally to a windswept hillock overlooking a fertile plain. There, the beast laid down to rest and there, too, following the oracle's instructions, Cadmus founded a city. He called it Cadmea, after himself. Later, the city became known as Thebes, while its highest point and fortress retained the founder's name.

Part of the founding ceremony involved sacrificing the cow that had led Cadmus into Boeotia. To perform the sacrifice, he needed water, so he sent his companions to a nearby stream. Unfortunately for these young men, the stream was guarded by a fierce serpent who, it was rumored, was the son of the war god, Ares. The serpent promptly killed and ate the men and when Cadmus saw what had happened, he angrily fought and slew the creature. According to one version of the story, Ares was so upset over the death of his serpentine son that he placed a curse on the succeeding generations of Cadmus's family. Another version maintains that Cadmus paid his debt to Ares by becoming the god's slave for a year.

In any case, soon after Cadmus had killed the serpent, Athena, goddess of wisdom, appeared before him. "Gather up the serpent's teeth and plant them in the earth," she advised. He did so, and not long afterward, to his surprise and fear, a small army of armed men sprang up from the furrows he had dug.[4] The earth-born men paid no attention to Cadmus, however. Instead, they furiously fought one another until only five of them were left; these survivors, whom Cadmus persuaded to become his helpers, became the founding fathers of Thebes's noble families.

CADMUS'S UNFORTUNATE DESCENDANTS

With the help of his new followers, Cadmus made Thebes a large and prosperous city, one that in time compared in power and prestige with Athens, Corinth, and other great Greek cities. Some say that Cadmus also introduced the alphabet, a Phoenician invention, to Greece. He married Harmonia, daughter of the god Ares and the goddess of love, Aphrodite. And thereafter, the royal couple enjoyed several years of happiness.

However, most of Cadmus's and Harmonia's children and grandchildren were not fated to be so happy and ended up having to endure one form of serious misfortune or another. One of their daughters, Semele, for instance, was accidentally incinerated by Zeus. At the time, she was pregnant with Zeus's son (who became the fertility god, Dionysus). Thanks to the intrigues of Hera, Zeus's jealous wife, Zeus paid a visit to Semele in the form of his symbol, the thunderbolt, killing her (although simultaneously making her child immortal).

Another daughter, Agave, had a son named Pentheus, who became king of Thebes (succeeding his grandfather, Cadmus). The young Dionysus became angry when Pentheus banned the god's followers from worshiping him in Thebes. So Dionysus made the city's women, Agave among them, wander through the countryside in a frenzied trance. Perceiving Pentheus as a lion or some other beast, they hunted him down and finally cornered him in a tree. In Euripides' *The Bacchae,* a messenger who witnessed what happened next states:

> Thousands of hands tore the fir tree from the earth, and down, down from his high perch fell Pentheus, tumbling to the ground, sobbing and screaming as he fell, for he knew his end was near. His own mother, like a priestess with her victim, fell upon him first. . . . "No, no, Mother!" [he screamed.] "I am Pentheus, your own son, the child you bore. . . . Pity me, spare me, Mother! I have done a wrong, but do not kill your own son for my offense." But she was foaming at the mouth, and her crazed eyes rolling with frenzy. . . . Ignoring his cries of pity, she seized his left arm at the wrist; then . . . pulled, wrenching away the arm at the shoulder. . . . The whole horde . . . swarmed upon him. . . . One tore off an arm, another a foot still warm in its shoe. His ribs were clawed clean of flesh and every hand was smeared with blood as they played ball with scraps of Pentheus' body.[5]

After this hideous incident, still another of Cadmus's daughters, Autonoe, had to endure her own son's death, which, unlike that of Pentheus, was quite undeserved. The following version of the demise of Autonoe's son, the unfortunate Actaeon, is by the noted modern myth-teller Edith Hamilton.

> He was out hunting and, hot and thirsty, entered a grotto where a little stream widened into a pool. He wanted only to cool himself in the crystal water. But all unknowing, he had chanced upon the favorite bathing place of Artemis [goddess of wild animals and the hunt]—and at the very moment when the goddess had let fall her garments and stood in her naked beauty on the water's edge. The offended divinity gave not a thought to whether the youth had purposely insulted her or had come there in all innocence. She flung into his face drops from her wet hand and as they fell upon him he

was changed into a stag. Not only outwardly. His heart became a deer's heart and he who had never known fear before was afraid and fled. His dogs saw him running and chased him. Even his agony of terror could not make him swift enough to outstrip the keen-scented pack. They fell upon him, his own faithful hounds, and killed him.[6]

ATTEMPTING TO SUBVERT DIVINE PROPHECY

After Pentheus's death, the Theban throne passed to Labdacus, who some ancient sources say was another of Cadmus's grandsons. Labdacus also died while pursuing unwise policies regarding Dionysian worship. His son, Laius, was only a small child at the time, so a nobleman named Lycus, who was a grandson of one of Cadmus's five earth-born men, assumed the role of regent, running the state for the young king. But soon Lycus got greedy and claimed the throne for himself. He ruled for twenty years, but received his just rewards when his own nephews, the twin brothers Amphion and Zethus, murdered him. The twins took over the city, banishing the rightful king, Laius, who was by now about twenty-one.

Many years passed and finally Amphion and Zethus died. This allowed Laius to return from exile and reclaim his throne. Once back in power, he married his distant cousin Jocasta, and not long afterward the Delphic oracle once more began playing a crucial role in the family's fortunes. Laius consulted the oracle about his own fate and received an answer that sorely dismayed him. "You and your new wife will have a son," the prophecy stated. "But be warned Laius: The son of whom I speak will one day slay you."

Because it was commonly held that Apollo's oracle never lied and that trying to change or get around one of its prophecies was both futile and an expression of distrust for the god, Laius was understandably fearful. But he was also arrogant. And despite warnings against trying to subvert the oracle, he grew determined to change the fate that had been decreed for him. When Jocasta bore him a son, he had the infant's feet bound together and ordered a servant to leave the child on the side of a mountain, where it would surely die. Confident that he had cheated fate, Laius breathed a sigh of relief and concentrated on ruling Thebes.

Many uneventful years passed. Then, the people of Thebes suddenly found themselves beset by a serious crisis.

A frightening monster began stalking the countryside around the city, a creature called the Sphinx, which had the body of a winged lion and the face of a human woman. The Sphinx would leap out at travelers and pose them a riddle; if a person could solve the riddle, the beast promised, it would let him or her go; if not, the Sphinx devoured the person alive. Because no one could solve the riddle, one Theban after another met doom in the creature's clutches and terror gripped the city. Making matters worse, news came that King Laius, now an old man, had been killed by robbers while traveling with some attendants along a road near Delphi. The widowed Jocasta and all of her subjects prayed to be delivered from their misery.

OEDIPUS SAVES THEBES

The Thebans' prayers seemed answered when a stalwart and intelligent young man named Oedipus, a traveler from the city of Corinth, appeared on the scene. He courageously confronted the monster, which naturally demanded that he solve the riddle. According to the first-century-B.C. Greek historian Diodorus Siculus,

> This is what was set forth by the Sphinx: "What is it that is of itself two-footed, three-footed, and four-footed?" Although the others could not see through it, Oedipus replied that the answer was "man," for as an infant man begins to move as a four-footed being [crawling on all fours], when he is grown he is two-footed, and as an old man he is three-footed, leaning upon a staff because of his weakness.[7]

Distraught over having been vanquished by a mere human, the Sphinx committed suicide. Thebes was saved and the grateful citizens welcomed Oedipus as their king. He married Jocasta, who bore him two sons, Polynices and Eteocles, and two daughters, Antigone and Ismene, and there followed many years of happiness and prosperity.

Eventually, however, the Thebans once more found themselves in a state of crisis. A terrible plague fell upon the land, a blight that killed plants, livestock, and people alike. Determined to help his people, Oedipus sent his brother-in-law Creon to Delphi to consult the oracle; surely, they reasoned, the healing god Apollo would offer some saving piece of advice for the ailing city. And sure enough, Creon returned from Delphi with good news. The oracle had proclaimed that the plague would be lifted if and when Laius's murderer was apprehended and punished. Oedipus took up this cause enthusiastically. In the play *Oedipus the King,* Sophocles had him say: "[I] will lend my support to avenging this crime against this land and the god as well. . . . I shall leave no stone unturned, for we shall succeed with the help of the god or be destroyed if we fail."[8]

But in his search for Laius's killer, Oedipus soon discovered some odd and disturbing information. First, he spoke with the blind prophet Teiresias. This highly revered old man had already lived for several generations, during which time he had given advice to many rulers. He had not been born blind. Supposedly, as a young man he was magically transformed into a woman and then back again into a man, so that he had the unique perspective of having felt both male and female emotions. Later, when Zeus and Hera asked Teiresias to mediate in a dispute they were having, Teiresias took Zeus's side. In retaliation, the angry Hera blinded Teiresias, but Zeus compensated for this loss by granting the man longevity and the gift of prophecy.

Thus, when Teiresias gave advice or predictions to people, they usually took what he said to heart. Teiresias told Oedipus that he, Oedipus, was the very culprit for whom the Thebans searched. "*You* are the murderer," declared Teiresias.

> *You* are the unholy defilement of this land. . . . You are a pitiful figure. . . . You, who have eyes, cannot see the evil in which you stand. . . . Do you even know who your parents are? Without knowing it, you are the enemy of your own flesh and blood, the dead below and the living here above. The double edged curse of your mother and father . . . shall one day drive you from this land. You see straight now but then you will see darkness. You will scream aloud on that day. . . . There is no man alive whose ruin will be more pitiful than yours.[9]

THE HORRIFYING TRUTH IS REVEALED

Oedipus knew about the old seer's reputation for right predictions. But at first the Theban king angrily dismissed Teiresias's words, thinking it ridiculous that he, Oedipus, could be the killer. Jocasta also rejected this idea. She explained to Oedipus that Laius had been murdered by robbers where three roads came together near Delphi; therefore, Oedipus was obviously not the guilty party. But on hearing his wife describe the specific location of the crime, Oedipus suddenly felt a small chill run up and down his spine. "When exactly did this happen?" he asked Jocasta. "Why, just before you arrived in Thebes," she answered casually.

Increasingly worried and uneasy, Oedipus proceeded to tell Jocasta about how he had come to Thebes in the first place. He had been the loving son of Corinth's king and queen, Polybus and Merope. Upon learning from the Delphic oracle that he was fated to kill his own father and marry his own mother, the horrified Oedipus had attempted to escape the prophecy by fleeing Corinth. If he never saw Polybus and Merope again, he reasoned, he could never end up killing one and marrying the other. Oedipus had struck out for Thebes, and in time, as he now told Jocasta,

> I came near to [a] triple crossroads and there I was met by a herald and a man riding on a horse-drawn wagon, just as you described it. The driver, and the old man himself, tried to push me off the road. In anger, I struck the driver. . . . When the old man saw me coming . . . he aimed at my head . . . and hit me. I paid him back in full. . . . I killed the whole lot of them.[10]

As Oedipus and Jocasta continued to talk, a messenger arrived from Corinth, bringing them the fateful news that old King Polybus had recently died. At first, it seemed as though this news proved that the oracle's pronouncements could indeed be false or avoided. After all, Polybus was dead and it was clear to all that Oedipus had had no hand in the deed, as the oracle had predicted he would. But then the Corinthian messenger stepped forward and told a story that made Oedipus shudder and Jocasta turn pale. Oedipus was not Polybus's son, said the messenger; Polybus and Merope had brought him up as their own after he, the messenger, had presented him to them. And where had he gotten the child? A servant of Thebes's King Laius had secretly given him the baby. Only minutes later, that very same servant, now an old man, confirmed the messenger's story. When Laius had ordered him to leave the baby outside to die, the servant had taken pity on it and given it to the Corinthian for safekeeping.

The horrifying truth was now clear to all. Oedipus was indeed, as Teiresias had earlier claimed, the guilty man who had brought the curse of the gods down on Thebes. Both Laius and Oedipus had tried to escape their fates and in so doing had sealed them. The prophecy that Laius would die by his own son's hand had been fulfilled, while the oracular prediction that Oedipus would murder his father and marry his mother had also come to pass.

Soon, Teiresias's own predictions, namely that Oedipus would scream aloud and see darkness, came true as well. Unable to cope with the horror of his acts, the Theban king wailed like a mortally wounded animal and in a fit of despair gouged out his own eyes. As for Jocasta, the realization that she had married her own son and had children by him was too much for her and she killed herself.

In this way, all involved learned the lesson that what the gods and fate decree no human can or should challenge. And Oedipus's fall from the heights of prosperity and happiness to the depths of wretchedness and despair illustrated another lesson—that suffering is an inevitable part of life and takes the ultimate measure of every person, rich or poor, mighty or humble. As Sophocles put it in the conclusion of *Oedipus the King:*

> O citizens of our native Thebes, behold: Here is Oedipus, who solved the renowned riddle and became ruler of our city and was regarded with envy by every citizen because of his good fortune. Think of the flood of terrible disaster that has swept over him. Thus, since we are all mortal, consider even a man's final day on earth and do not pronounce him happy until he has crossed the finish line of life without the pain of suffering.[11]

OEDIPUS'S FATE AND POLYNICES' ATTACK ON THEBES

After Oedipus's terrible realization and Jocasta's suicide, Oedipus resigned the Theban throne and soon afterward suffered banishment. In most people's eyes he was cursed, a polluted figure condemned to wander aimlessly from one city to another and be rejected by each. Only his daughters, Antigone and Ismene, remained faithful to and cared for him. To help guide the blind man, Antigone traveled with him, while Ismene remained in Thebes and kept him informed from time to time of events in his former home. Meanwhile, Jocasta's brother, Creon (who was, under the circumstances, both brother-in-law and uncle to Oedipus), became regent in Thebes, managing the city for Polynices and Eteocles, who were still too young to rule.

After wandering for several years, Oedipus and Antigone arrived at Colonus, a village on the outskirts of Athens. The Athenian king, Theseus, kindly allowed the fallen ruler to stay. This benefited both Oedipus, who now enjoyed a friendly, comfortable refuge, and Athens, since the newest of Apollo's prophecies stated that the gods would grant blessings and prosperity to the land bearing Oedipus's last resting place. Ismene traveled to Colonus to inform her father of this prophecy. There, she and Antigone remained with him until he died, or more accurately, until he mysteriously disappeared. The gods, it appears, had accepted him into their bosom and made him immortal, for in their eyes he had suffered enough; moreover, in bringing good fortune to Athens, he had redeemed himself and become a hero once more.

Oedipus's troubles were finally over. But the same cannot be said for his unfortunate offspring. Antigone and Ismene returned to Thebes to find the city embroiled in still another crisis, this one instigated by Oedipus's sons. Polynices and Eteocles had recently come of age and had argued angrily about which of them should rule Thebes. They finally struck a deal, agreeing that Eteocles would rule for a year while his brother went into exile, after which Polynices would rule for a year while Eteocles went away, and so forth.

Once Eteocles had assumed power, however, it quickly became clear that he had no intention of keeping his end of the bargain. Deciding that he must resort to force to drive his brother from the throne, Polynices enlisted the aid of six noble warriors from the Greek city of Argos. Each of the Argive army's seven commanders (counting Polynices) attacked one of Thebes's seven well-fortified gates, but after long rounds of bloody battle, they failed to penetrate the city's walls. Finally, both sides agreed that the war should be decided by single combat, namely a fight to the death between the rival leaders—Polynices and Eteocles. No one could have predicted the tragic outcome, about which a messenger tells the Chorus of Theban women in Aeschylus's *Seven Against Thebes:*

MESSENGER: The town is safe. But the two sons of Oedipus—

CHORUS: What of them? I am bewildered—I am afraid to hear. . . .

MESSENGER: Both are dead. They killed each other.

CHORUS: Each too much like his brother in the lust to kill.

MESSENGER: Each like the other in the fate that led them both, the fate which now annihilates their ill-starred race. . . . So, Thebes is saved. But her two brother kings are fallen; the earth has drunk their blood, shed by each other's hands.[12]

With Eteocles dead, his uncle, Creon, assumed the Theban throne. He gave orders that, in retaliation for the brutal attack on the city, the Argive dead, including Polynices, should be forbidden proper burial. And it is with this proclamation and Antigone's heartfelt reaction to it that the events depicted in Sophocles' *Antigone* begin.

NOTES

1. Over time, the Trojan myths were collected into several large epic poems, including the *Cypria, Iliad, Aethiopis, Little Iliad, Homecomings, Odyssey,* and *Telogony.* Of these, only the *Iliad* and *Odyssey,* attributed to the legendary eighth-century (?) poet Homer, have survived. Worthwhile translations are Robert Fagles' version of the *Iliad* (New York: Penguin Books, 1990) and E.V. Rieu's version of the *Odyssey* (Baltimore: Penguin Books, 1961). For commentary and other information, see Don Nardo, ed., *Readings on Homer.* San Diego: Greenhaven Press, 1998.

2. For all three of Sophocles' Theban plays in one volume, see Robert Fagles, trans., *Sophocles: The Three Theban Plays:* Antigone, Oedipus the King, Oedipus at Colonus. New York: Penguin Books, 1984. Bernard M.W. Knox's translation of *Oedipus the King* (New York: Pocket Books, 1959) is also highly regarded. For Aeschylus's *Seven Against Thebes,* see Philip Vellacott, trans., *Aeschylus:* Prometheus Bound, The Suppliants, Seven Against Thebes, The Persians. Baltimore: Penguin Books, 1961. And for Euripides' Theban plays, see David Grene and Richmond Lattimore, eds., *Euripides III:* Orestes, Iphigenia in Aulis, Electra, The Phoenician Women, The Bacchae. New York: Random House, 1959.

3. Actually, not just one, but a long succession of priestesses bore the title of oracle. The term also referred to the shrine itself, as well as to an answer given by the priestess.

4. In another Greek myth, which tells of the adventures of the hero Jason and his ship, the *Argo,* the serpent's teeth sown by Cadmus crop up again. In Jason's story, Aeëtes, king of the land of Colchis, has in his possession a few of Cadmus's seeds (which for some reason did not germinate when Cadmus planted them), as well as the much-prized Golden Fleece. Aeëtes claims he will surrender the Fleece to Jason if Jason will use two fire-breathing bronze bulls to plow the teeth into a field. Jason does so and, as in Cadmus's story, armed men spring up from the furrows.

5. Grene's and Lattimore's translation (see above), pp. 407–408.

6. *Mythology.* New York: New American Library, 1942, pp. 255–56.

7. *Library of History,* quoted in Rhoda A. Hendricks, ed. and trans., *Classical Gods and Heroes: Myths as Told by the Ancient Authors.* New York: Morrow Quill, 1974, p. 108.

8. Quoted in Hendricks, *Classical Gods and Heroes,* pp. 113–14.

9. Sophocles, *Oedipus the King,* Knox's translation (see note #2), pp. 23, 25, 28–29.

10. *Oedipus the King,* Knox's translation, pp. 56–57.

11. Quoted in Hendricks, *Classical Gods and Heroes,* p. 152.

12. Vellacott's translation (see note #2), pp. 112–13.

CHAPTER 1

The Plot, Themes, and Ideas of *Antigone*

The Story of *Antigone*

Michael Grant

This overview of the plot of Sophocles' *Antigone*
is by the renowned and prolific classical historian
Michael Grant. As Grant explains, the action of the
play takes place in and around the Theban palace
once ruled by Oedipus, father of Antigone, Ismene,
Polynices, and Eteocles. In the first two plays in
Sophocles' Oedipus saga, *Oedipus the King* and
Oedipus at Colonus, Oedipus tragically falls from
power and grace and disappears. He leaves behind
two willful sons, an equally willful daughter
(Antigone), and an ambitious father-in-law (Creon),
who proceed to entwine themselves in a tragedy of
their own.

Out of the Theban palace—formerly the home of their father
Oedipus—Antigone and her sister Ismene appear. Thebes
has recently been besieged by an Argive army led by the
Seven; their chief was the girls' exiled brother Polynices,
whose brother Eteocles had driven him out of the city in order that he himself might be sole king. The two men have
killed one another in single combat, but the invaders were
thrown back, and now Antigone reveals to her sister a fateful edict pronounced by their uncle King Creon. For Creon
has decreed that only Eteocles should receive honourable
burial. The corpse of Polynices, on the other hand, since he
has shown himself the enemy of his country, is to be thrown
out and left lying in the plain, a prey for the birds. The
penalty for anyone who attempts to bury him is death.

ANTIGONE CONDEMNED

Antigone tells her sister she is determined to disobey this
impious order, and appeals to Ismene to help her. But Ismene does not dare to agree, and Antigone casts her off—
"since apparently the laws of the gods mean nothing to you."

The chorus of Theban elders enter and tell the story of the war, naming Polynices as the aggressor and describing how he and his brother met in duel and fell. Creon appears and informs the elders of his edict, declaring it a reward for patriotism and a penalty for treason. His hearers acquiesce—

> For you can make such rulings as you will
> About the living and about the dead . . .
> What other order would you give us, then?

> CREON: Not to take sides with any who disobey.
> CHORUS: No fool is fool as far as loving death.

Nevertheless, a guard now arrives with the news that some unidentified person has already carried out funeral rites for Polynices, by performing the symbolic act of sprinkling dust upon his body. Creon dismisses the guard with threats of a horrible fate if he does not find those who have committed this treasonable deed. But the action prompts the elders to meditate upon man's daring and inventiveness and resource, which bring him triumph if he obeys divine and human laws, but ruin if he disregards them.

> Words also, and thought as rapid as air,
> He fashions to his good use; statecraft is his,
> And his the skill that deflects the arrows of snow,
> The spears of winter rain. From every wind
> He has made himself secure—from all but one:
> In the late wind of death he cannot stand.

> O clear intelligence, force beyond all measure!
> O fate of man, working both good and evil!
> When the laws are kept, how proudly his city stands!
> When the laws are broken, what of his city then?
> Never may the anarchic man find rest at my hearth,
> Never be it said that my thoughts are his thoughts.

But they break off in distress as Antigone herself is led in by the guard. Interrogated by Creon, she answers that she knew of his decree, but had nevertheless paid burial honours to her brother Polynices because she believed that no human law can rise above the laws of heaven. Compared to these, she declares, her death is of no importance. Creon swears that she shall indeed die a dreadful death. Ismene, whom he likewise suspects, is now brought in, and begs to die with her sister who refuses her plea, however, as "unjust." Ismene then urges Creon to reprieve Antigone, but fails, even when she appeals to Antigone's betrothal to his own son Haemon. Creon sends the sisters into the palace as prisoners, denouncing both of them. The elders speak of the grim fate which has cursed the royal house of Thebes, one generation after another. But any greatness in human life, they add, brings doom, and the victims of those tricked by hope know nothing until they have walked into the flames.

THE POWER OF LOVE

Haemon enters, to plead with his father Creon for the life of his destined bride. He argues with restraint, and shows solicitousness for his father's position. But after receiving angry and stinging rebukes in reply, he goes away, telling Creon they will never see each other again. The king then discloses to the chorus what kind of death he has decided for Antigone.

> To take her where the foot of man comes not.
> There shall I hide her in a hollowed cave
> Living, and leave her just so much to eat
> As clears the city from the guilt of death.

The elders, however, choose this moment to celebrate the power of love, and to stress that none can resist it: for love was what caused this present quarrel between kinsmen. When Antigone is taken out by Creon's servants, on their way to the tomb, the chorus declare that her death will bring her renown. She compares her fate to that of Niobe, daughter of Tantalus, who, after Apollo and Artemis had killed all her children, was turned to stone from weeping. But the elders attribute her end to her own overboldness, which has dashed her heavily against the lofty pedestal of Justice.

> You showed respect for the dead.
> So we for you: but power
> Is not to be thwarted so.
> Your self-sufficiency has brought you down.

As Creon returns and orders her to be immured forthwith, Antigone asserts her belief in the loving welcome she will find from her father, mother and brother beyond the grave. "The wise," she says, "will know my choice was right"—for even children or a husband could have been replaced, but never her brother, for whom she had performed this final service. She cries out asking what divine justice she has disobeyed, and which of the gods she can call her ally: for it is they who will judge whether she or the other side are wrong. Antigone is sent away, and the chorus, thinking of her rocky tomb, sing of Danaë who was immured by her father Acrisius of Argos but visited by Zeus in golden rain; of Lycurgus who raged at Dionysus and was pent in a rock-walled prison; and of Cleopatra—daughter of Boreas, and wife of Thracian Phineus—whom Idothea, taken by her husband in her place, so hated that she put out the eyes of Cleopatra's two sons.

THE LIVING AMONG THE DEAD

Led in by a boy, the old, blind prophet Tiresias has an urgent warning for the king. The omens show that the gods are angry with Thebes, and the king's edict is the cause of this taint.

> All of the altars of the town are choked
> With leavings of the dogs and birds; their feast
> Was on that fated, fallen Polynices.
> So the gods will have no offering from us,
> Not prayer, nor flame of sacrifice. The birds
> Will not cry out a sound I can distinguish,
> Gorged with the greasy blood of that dead man . . .
> Yield to the dead!

Creon furiously refuses to abandon his plan, charging Tiresias with complicity in a plot fomented by seditious Thebans. This goads the prophet into declaring that Creon shall pay with his own son's life for his double sin: the detention of the dead among the living, and the imprisonment of the living among the dead. He leaves, but Creon is shaken, for he, like the chorus, has never known a prophecy of Tiresias to be wrong.

So the king decides to give way. He sets out with his servants for the plain, to bury the dead and set his niece free, while the elders pray joyfully that Dionysus may come with healing power to his beloved Thebes.

But one of his companions soon returns with a report, which is heard by the king's wife Eurydice. After burning the remains of Polynices, Creon has found Antigone dead, by her own hand. Haemon was embracing her corpse, and his father appealed to him to come away.

> The boy looked at him with his angry eyes,
> Spat in his face and spoke no further word.
> He drew his sword, but as his father ran,
> He missed his aim. Then the unhappy boy,
> In anger at himself, leant on the blade.

Eurydice passes silently into the house, and Creon enters with attendants carrying Haemon's body on a bier. As the king laments, a messenger announces that Eurydice has stabbed herself beside the altar, her last words a curse upon Creon the slayer of her children. Creon prays frantically to die, but the elders can only tell him that no mortal escapes the doom prepared for him, and that great words by proud men are punished by great blows.

The Play Is a Treasure Trove of Western Cultural Principles

Victor D. Hanson and John Heath

Underlying and supporting the story and major themes of *Antigone* are numerous political and cultural concepts and ideals that are peculiarly Greek and which have become a part of Western civilization's fabric. This masterful examination of these principles and their relation to the action of the play is by Victor D. Hanson, professor of Greek at California State University at Fresno, and John Heath, chairman of the classics department at Santa Clara University.

The answer to why the world is becoming Westernized goes all the way back to the wisdom of the Greeks.... Our own implicit principles and values can be rediscovered in... Sophocles' tragedy *Antigone* (441 B.C.), produced at the zenith of Athenian imperial power and cultural hegemony. Within a mere 1,353 lines one can detect most of the cultural assumptions of all the Greeks that we now 2,500 years later take for granted—even though Sophocles' tragedy is an exploration of civic and private morality, *not* a treatise on culture. In other words, a piece of Athenian literature, otherwise ostensibly *unconcerned* with political science or cultural studies, can serve as an effective primer to anyone curious about how we are like the Greeks in our daily lives. If we put aside for a moment the *Antigone* as great literature and examine the nuts and bolts of its underlying assumptions about man and culture, the play can be as revealing from the values it presumes as from the tensions it raises and the ideas it challenges.

BACKGROUND NOISES OF THE DRAMA

The play's heroine is Antigone, sister and daughter of the dead Oedipus. She opposes a royal edict forbidding burial of her brother, Polyneices, the defeated usurper of Thebes, who had tried to wrest the kingdom from his own brother. Forced either to follow the law or her own notions of universal morality and sisterly duty, Antigone attempts to give burial rites to Polyneices. This pious but illegal act earns her a death sentence. A Sophoclean calamity follows for her uncle, the regent king Creon, who would punish her for traitorous conduct. Creon's increasingly tyrannical behavior in pursuit of the law—fear and rejection of family, fellow citizens, and the divine—results in the death of his son, his wife, and Antigone herself. The state and its smug assurance that statute can challenge divinely inspired custom seem to go too far, with disastrous consequences for all involved.

Within this single drama—in great part, a harsh critique of Athenian society and the Greek city-state in general—Sophocles tells of the eternal struggle between the state and the individual, human and natural law, and the enormous gulf between what we attempt here on earth and what fate has in store for us all. In this magnificent dramatic work, almost incidentally so, we find nearly every reason why we are now what we are. The following categories taken from the play by no means exhaust the Western paradigm [pattern of cultural ideas and principles]. They are, again, *not* even the chief reasons to read the tragedy; they are simply the background noises of the drama. These underlying cultural assumptions, however . . . illuminate much about our own lives in the West at the turn of the millennium.

SCIENCE, RESEARCH, AND THE ACQUISITION OF KNOWLEDGE ITSELF ARE TO REMAIN APART FROM BOTH RELIGIOUS AND POLITICAL AUTHORITY

To the Greeks, the free exchange of ideas, the abstract and rational inquiry about the physical and material world, and the pursuit of knowledge for its own sake create a dynamic that is both brilliant and frightening at the same time—and unlike that of any other culture. The chorus of Theban elders in a triumphant ode sing of the progress of technology in its mastery over nature. There are "many wondrous things and nothing more wondrous than man," whose naval, agricultural, medical, and manufacturing sciences have conquered everything but death itself. Armed with his dangerous "inventive craft," *polis* man—that is, the citizen of the city-state—can apply his mechanical skill (*techné*) "beyond all expectation," and use it "for either evil or good," a potent scientific enterprise whose goal is progress itself at any cost. It is no wonder that the troubled Sophocles chooses to use the ambiguous adjective *deina* for "wondrous." The Greek word is more akin to the English "awful," or "formidable" and means both wonderful and terrible—astonishingly good *or* strange and unusual to the point of being terribly bad.

To Sophocles, who experienced the splendor and precipitous decline of imperial Athens in the fifth century, and who recognized the role of both divine fate and mortal hubris in its descent, there is always a price to be paid for relentless human progress that, in [his playwright colleague] Euripides' words, makes "us arrogant in claiming that we are better than the Gods." Anyone who has witnessed our mountains denuded of primeval forests so that the lower middle classes might have clean, affordable, and durable tract houses recognizes the technological and ethical trade-off that Sophocles worried about.

MILITARY POWER OPERATES UNDER AND IS CHECKED BY CIVILIAN CONTROL

Throughout the *Antigone*, the would-be usurper Polyneices is condemned for raising an army outside the law to gain control of Thebes. Moreover, Creon's guards serve not as retainers—who may bolt and change sides when their king's fortunes wane—but rather as reluctant militiamen who enforce legislation that they do not necessarily like. Nowhere is their "general" a divine prince. These men-at-arms therefore can freely offer advice, even speak rudely if need be, to their commander-in-chief, who exercises power solely by his position as the legal head of the state. The Guard, in fact, rebukes Creon for his rash and unsubstantiated charges: "How terrible to guess, and to guess at untruths!" Sophocles was writing within a society where almost every elected Greek general was at some time either fined, exiled, ostracized, or executed, where almost every commander fought beside his men and hardly a one survived when his army did not. The playwright himself both led men into battle and served as auditor of others who had failed. No one in Sophocles' audience would have thought it at all strange for a soldier to question his leader or for a lowly private to be a wiser man than his general. As Aristotle reminds us of Athens, "All offices connected with the military are to be elected by an open vote."

CONSTITUTIONAL AND CONSENSUAL GOVERNMENT IS A WESTERN IDEA

The idea of constitutional government permeates every aspect of the *Antigone.* Although the Greek tragedians anachronistically use the conventions of early myth and thus the dramatic architecture from the pre–city-state world of kings and clans, much of the *Antigone* is about contradictions within law, government, and jurisprudence—issues very much at stake in Sophocles' own fifth-century world of Athens. The poet transforms the mythical monarchy of Thebes into a veritable contemporary city-state, where citizens must make legislation and yet live with that majority decision even when it is merely legal and not at all ethical or moral. Creon must announce the edict "to the whole people." Antigone and her sister Ismene acknowledge that burying their brother and thus breaking the law of the *polis* is illegal and therefore "against the citizens." When Creon boasts of his power to enforce the state's edict, his own son Haemon is made to counter, "No *polis* is the property of a single man." No city-state—even the more oligarchical—really was.

Creon himself turns out to be a tragic figure, an utterly Western rational creature who devotes himself to the law above every other human and divine concern. He is tragic in his own right not just because he goes against the moral consensus of his own citizenry and the wishes of the gods, but because he does so in the sincere belief that as head of state he is adhering to a necessary Greek sense of consensual government—something which exists only, in Aristotle's words, "when the citizens rule and are then ruled in turn."

RELIGION IS SEPARATE FROM AND SUBORDINATE TO POLITICAL AUTHORITY

In the Greek city-state, no high priest is invested with absolute political authority. This separation of roles will . . . establish an ideal that would serve reformers for the next two and a half millennia. The council and assembly govern political and military affairs—stage elections, vote on legislation, appoint generals, call out the militias, expect the citizens, not the state, to provide arms. In the age of the classical city-state, no free citizen curtsies or kowtows to a living deity. Prophets, seers, and priests conduct festivals, sacrifices, advise, counsel, and interpret the supernatural; they do not *per se* direct state policy or override the will of the assembly. The archon is not God incarnate, who marries his sister, leads his people in public prayer and sacrifice, oversees the building of his monumental tomb, or sits on a peacock throne. The holy man may threaten or mesmerize in his attempts to sway the assembly, but sway the assembly he must.

Thus in the *Antigone,* the seer Teiresias, who through his supernatural craft possesses greater wisdom than Creon, nevertheless is slandered ("The whole pack of seers is money-mad") and arbitrarily dismissed by the king. When he is told to leave, he goes. It is not Creon's sacrilegious abuse of the holy man Teiresias that dooms him; rather it is his paranoia and political extremism in rejecting the sound, rational advice of family and friend alike. No Greek would think that Teiresias deserved a veto or that Creon could read the signs of birds. Plato saw the holy man and the statesman as distinct; "the diviner arrogant with pride and influence" was not to intrude into government, "as in Egypt, where the King cannot rule unless he has the power of a priest."

TRUSTING NEITHER THE RICH NOR THE POOR, THE GREEKS OF THE *POLIS* HAVE GREAT FAITH IN THE AVERAGE CITIZEN (THE SPIRITUAL FORERUNNER OF OUR OWN CONFIDENCE IN THE MIDDLE CLASS)

The yeoman farmer, the shepherd, the small craftsmen, the nurse, the citizen-soldier—these are the unsung heroes of Greek tragic and comic drama. These secondary but essential characters and chorus members provide the stable backdrop for the murder, incest, and madness of a royal and divine mythical elite who live in a different world from the rest of us. At the very origins of Western culture, Greece created an anti-aristocratic ethos often hostile to the accumulation of riches, and to the entire notion of the wealthy man of influence—and it is one of the few societies in the history of civilization to have done so.

The Greeks were more naturally suspicious than admiring of plutocratic hierarchy, indeed of anything that threatened the decentralized nature of the *polis,* which is the natural expression of a community of peers. Haemon warns his father Creon of the public rumbling over Antigone's death sentence, of the need to consider the opinion of the "common man," "the people who share our city." In the *Antigone* of Sophocles (himself the well-born son of a wealthy manufacturer), the populist streak runs strong in almost every direction—economic, social, and political. Creon himself rails against the power of money: "You will see more people destroyed than saved by dirty profits." Earlier he had concluded, "Men are ruined by the hope of profit."

Both Sophocles and Euripides endow their middling messengers, guards, farmers, heralds, caretakers, and shepherds with a refreshing degree of common sense; they are wily, astute, sensitive, rarely naive, rarely buffoons. The

THE GREEK RULE OF LAW

In this excerpt from his famed funeral oration (as recounted by the Greek historian Thucydides in his history of the Peloponnesian War), the Athenian statesman Pericles boasts that his city's democratic system affords its citizens unprecedented freedom and justice.

"Our constitution does not copy the laws of neighboring states; we are rather a pattern to others than imitators ourselves. Its administration favors the many instead of the few; this is why it is called a democracy. If we look to the laws, they afford equal justice to all in their private differences; if to social standing, advancement in public life falls to reputation for capacity, class considerations not being allowed to interfere with merit; nor again does poverty bar the way, if a man is able to serve the state, he is not hindered by the obscurity of his condition. The freedom which we enjoy in our government extends also to our ordinary life. There, far from exercising a jealous surveillance over each other, we do not feel called upon to be angry with our neighbor for doing what he likes, or even to indulge in those injurious looks which cannot fail to be offensive, although they inflict no real harm. But all this ease in our private relations does not make us lawless as citizens. Against this fear is our chief safeguard, teaching us to obey the magistrates and the laws, particularly such as regard the protection of the injured, whether they are actually on the statute book, or belong to that code which, although unwritten, yet cannot be broken without acknowledged disgrace."

Thucydides, *The Peloponnesian War*, published as *The Landmark Thucydides: A Comprehensive Guide to the Peloponnesian War*. Trans. Richard Crawley, ed. Robert B. Strassler. New York: Simon and Schuster, 1996, p. 170.

messenger in the *Antigone* dryly concludes of the royal fiasco, "Enjoy your wealth; live the life of a king; but once your enjoyment has left, these are but the shadows of smoke in comparison to lost happiness." No wonder the play ends with, "Great words of the haughty bring great blows upon them"—words that would have cost a Persian of those times his head. In short, Sophocles was drawing on a rich anti-aristocratic tradition of the previous two centuries . . . [that revels in] exposing the ugly side of the rich and famous. Sophocles' contemporary Thucydides has Athenagoras say of the people's ability to govern that the wealthy are fit only as guardians of property, while "the many, they are the best judges of what is spoken."

PRIVATE PROPERTY AND FREE ECONOMIC ACTIVITY ARE IMMUNE FROM GOVERNMENT COERCION AND INTERFERENCE

In the world of the Greek city-state, the citizen has title to his own property, the right to inherit and to pass on what is rightfully his. That decentralized system explains why the Greeks colonized—and often exploited—the Eastern and southern Mediterranean rather than vice versa. But in contrast to the earlier palatial dynasties to the East and South, taxation and the forced labor of the free citizenry were nearly nonexistent. Creon, like so many Greek rightists from the sixth-century B.C. aristocrat Theognis to Plato, railed against the rise of capital and commerce among the citizenry, which had destroyed the allocation of wealth and power by birth alone, to the detriment of his own inherited, entrenched position: "No practice is as pernicious among the citizenry as coined money. It destroys the state; it drives men from their homes; it teaches men vice in order to abandon good sense in favor of shameful deeds." Wealth without proof of morality upsets static norms of social behavior and established political power, disrupting old hierarchies as well as the obedience and compliance of the populace.

In short, the free market—even the Greeks' less-developed, protocapitalist one—erodes inherited privilege, allowing a different and changeable standard of merit, based on achievement, to prevail. When Athenian democracy is either scorned by the Old Oligarch (the name given to the author of a fifth-century treatise denouncing Athenian democracy) or praised by Pericles himself, the focus is often on the harbor and agora, the loci of free trade and commerce which empower the mob and give flesh to the abstract promise of equality.

The Notion of Dissent and Open Criticism of Government, Religion, and the Military Is Inherent Among the *Polis* Greeks

Anywhere else in the Mediterranean the loud-mouthed, hell-raising troublemaker is shunned, beheaded, or transmogrified into the court toady. In the Greek world the dissident—Ajax, Philoctetes, Lysistrata, Electra, Prometheus [title characters of famous ancient Greek plays]—often becomes the eponymous hero of the play. Antigone attacks Greek culture on a variety of fronts—the tyranny of the state over the individual, the mindless chauvinism of a male supremacist, the complacence and passivity of timid citizenry, the relativism of a more modern world growing insidiously in her midst. She warns that no mortal, even with the law of the state at his side, "could trample down the unwritten and unfailing laws of the gods." Head-to-head in a moral debate with Creon, she pushes the king to the shallow refuge of sexual bias. Exasperated, he can only bluster: "No woman rules me while I live." When Antigone's more circumspect and fence-sitting sister Ismene finally decides to participate in the burial, she receives from Antigone a cold "No": "I cannot love a friend whose love is words."

One could argue that Sophocles himself wants to undermine the very *polis* that allows him to present his dramas, that he uses his state subsidy to convince his Athenian patrons that their problem, the cause of their decline, is in *them*, not in the gods, women, foreigners, slaves, or other Greeks. His contemporary Pericles says of such free speech that it is "not a stumbling block but rather a vital precursor for any action at all."

The Maltreatment of a Human Body Evokes Horror and Outrage

H.D.F. Kitto

The late H.D.F. (Humphry Davy Findly) Kitto (1897–1982) was one of the twentieth century's leading authorities on Greek tragedy. Although fascinated by all of Sophocles' surviving works, *Antigone* held a special place in his heart, as evidenced by his request that the readings at his funeral be taken from its choral odes. This is his brief but forceful analysis of a major theme of the play—the dispute over whether a human body should be given a decent burial. Kitto makes the point that it is not the nature of ancient Greek religious beliefs about the soul that make this theme relevant to all people in all ages. It is rather the "indecent outrage" any person will feel and express when the body of a friend or relative is treated with disrespect.

Those who write about the *Antigone* tend to be rather apologetic on this matter [proper burial]. It was believed by the Greeks that unless a body was buried, literally or symbolically, the soul of the dead man could not find rest in Hades; this explains why such importance is given, in this play, to the burial of Polyneices. It is remarkable how many commentators have told us this; remarkable, because one has only to read the play to see that it contains not a single word about the peace of Polyneices' soul. But that would be taken for granted; matters of common knowledge or belief are tacitly assumed between dramatist and audience.

WHAT *IS* AND *ISN'T* IN THE PLAY

This doctrine of 'tacit assumption' is extremely dangerous to criticism. Up to a certain point it is obviously true: if a

Reprinted from H.D.F. Kitto, *Form and Meaning in Drama: A Study of Six Greek Plays and of "Hamlet"* (London: Methuen, 1956), by permission of Methuen and Company.

dramatist tells us that his hero has lost a leg, he will not add that he has only one left, however important that fact may be to his plot. But it is certainly not true that matters of common knowledge necessarily *are* assumed. In the theatre we look after ourselves; the critic has to use his judgment, and be careful. As to the present matter, we can produce a dozen or more passages from up and down Greek literature to prove that this belief existed—but what of that? If we say that Sophocles believed it, we are saying what we do not know;

TRADITIONAL GREEK BURIALS

Here, from his book Religion in Greece and Rome, *H.J. Rose, a noted authority on ancient religion, tells how the Greeks traditionally buried their dead.*

When one of the ancient Greeks came to die, his funeral ceremonies might be quite elaborate; we hear of sundry laws forbidding extravagant shows of grief and ostentatious expense at a burial. The funeral followed the death quickly, partly no doubt because the climate of Greece is warm and decomposition would soon set in, but perhaps even more because a dead man or woman has no business in this world, and the sooner he goes to his own place the better. The ceremonies began with the "laying out" (*próthesis*) of the corpse, which was neatly dressed and placed on a bed. Around it took place one of the most ancient of rites, the formal wailing, conducted by the women of the family, who might be led by specialists in the art of lamentation; regularly they had a leader of some sort, and the rest joined in a sort of chorus of grief. . . . The next stage was the funeral procession *(ekphorá,* literally carrying out), when the body, still on the bed, dressed usually in white and wearing a garland of some plant considered appropriate to the occasion, was carried to the burial-place, oftener than not outside the settlement. Here it was either burned and the ashes stored in an urn, which was then buried, or put unburned into a tomb or grave, often enclosed in a coffin. . . . If an unburied corpse was found, the finder could discharge his minimum duties towards it by sprinkling it with a little dust. . . .

Returning from the funeral, the mourners ate the funeral feast (*perídeipnon*) and purified themselves, washing off the taint of death. Their regular offerings at the tomb followed on the third and ninth days after the death, and in some places at least there was an annual rite, called at Athens *genésia*, the clan-feast.

H.J. Rose, *Religion in Greece and Rome.* New York: Harper and Brothers, 1959.

and if we bring it into our interpretation of the play, we are adding to the play something which demonstrably is not there, with the usual result: we are making it more difficult to notice what *is* there. The demonstration is simple. Negatively, not a single word is said about Polyneices' soul. Positively, there are several moments in the play when Antigone, passionately, even desperately, tells us why she had to bury him, whatever the cost. Are we then to suppose that the most compelling reason of all, the eternal peace of her brother's soul, was 'tacitly assumed'? . . .

DEVOURED BY BIRDS AND DOGS

The intrusive idea pushes something else out. What Sophocles emphasises, time after time, is the mangling of Polyneices' body. Antigone says to Ismene (26 ff): 'But Polyneices' body must lie, unlamented and unburied, a rich store of meat for hungry birds.' Creon says (198 ff): 'None shall give him burial. No; he shall lie unburied, his body devoured by birds and dogs, a foul sight to see.' The next reference comes in Haemon's speech. He reports the common people as saying: 'Has she not done a most glorious thing? When her own brother was slain and lay unburied, did not she save him from being destroyed by hungry birds and dogs?' Finally, we may note the grim detail in the messenger-speech: 'We buried what little was left.'

This is a dramatic fact, and I suggest that it is an important one. It is clearly one which we must take into account when we are considering Antigone's motives. It is perhaps even more important, that it makes it quite unnecessary for us, when we are introducing the *Antigone* to new readers, to remark by way of preface: 'You must understand, and take for granted, that the Greeks had certain religious ideas, foreign to us, about the burial of the dead.' So perhaps they did, but the fact is irrelevant and misleading. What Sophocles relies on and presents again and again is the sheer physical horror, the sense of indecent outrage, that we all feel, modern [people] as well as ancient Greek [people], at the idea that a human body, the body of someone we have known and maybe loved, should be treated like this.

The Play Dramatizes Problems Faced by Politicians

Edith Hall

According to this essay by Edith Hall, lecturer in classics at England's University of Reading, a major theme of *Antigone* is the indecisive manner in which a politician (Creon) deals with a serious crisis. In Hall's view, Creon is incapable of separating his private relationships from his state duties and powers. And this leads him to make the wrong decisions, which, in turn, lead to tragedy.

Of all Sophocles' tragedies *Antigone* is the most overtly political, in that it directly confronts problems involved in running a *polis,* a city-state. The ancients already recognized this; a tradition emerged that Sophocles' election to the generalship in 441/0 was a direct result of the success of the play. In modern times the political element has inspired numerous adaptations and productions, often anachronistically portraying Antigone as a liberal individualist shaking her little fist against a totalitarian state: she has been made to protest against everything from Nazism (especially in the versions by Jean Anouilh of 1944 and Bertolt Brecht of 1948) to eastern-bloc communism, South African apartheid, and British imperialism in Ireland.

LAWGIVING REVEALS ONE'S CHARACTER?

The action of the play . . . is set in Thebes, a mainland Greek city-state to the north of Athens and in reality antidemocratic and hostile to her; the Athenian dramatists typically displaced or 'expatriated' to Thebes political strife, tyranny, and domestic chaos. *Antigone* opens at a moment of political crisis caused directly by internecine warfare [i.e., civil war]. King Oedipus and Iocasta, now deceased, had

Excerpted from Introduction, by Edith Hall, ©1994 by Edith Hall, to *Sophocles: "Antigone," "Oedipus the King," "Electra,"* edited by Edith Hall, translated by H.D.F. Kitto (Oxford: Oxford University Press, 1994), translations ©1962 by Oxford University Press. Reprinted by permission of Oxford University Press.

four children, Polyneices, Eteocles, Antigone, and Ismene. The two sons quarrelled over the kingship of Thebes, and Polyneices was driven into exile; Eteocles was left ruling Thebes, apparently with the support of the brothers' maternal uncle Creon. Polyneices formed an alliance with the king of the important Peloponnesian city of Argos . . . and raised a force with which to attack his own city. The assault failed, but in the battle Polyneices and Eteocles killed each other.

The tragedy begins at dawn after the Theban victory; Creon, as the nearest surviving male relative of the two sons of Oedipus, has now assumed power. The play enacts the catastrophic events which take place on his first day in office; it ironically demonstrates the truth of his own inaugural speech, in which he pronounces that no man's character can be known 'Until he has been proved by government | And lawgiving.' For the very first law which Creon passes—that the body of the traitor Polyneices is to be refused burial—is in direct contravention of the 'Unwritten Law' protecting the rights of the dead; it precipitates, moreover, not only the death of his disobedient niece Antigone, who buries the corpse, but also the suicides of his own son Haemon and of Creon's wife Eurydice.

AN INCONSISTENT POLITICIAN

Antigone explores the difficult path any head of state must tread between clear leadership and despotism. It has sometimes been argued that Creon's law was defensible, given the divisive nature of the civil war which had blighted Thebes and the urgent need for a firm hand on the rudder of government. Funerals, as politicians everywhere know, can spark off insurrection. It is even possible to see Creon's failure to achieve heroic stature, at least in human terms, as a result simply of his unsteadiness in the face of opposition. For he is, above all, erratic: having decided that Ismene is as guilty as Antigone, he then changes his mind about her. He vacillates wildly about Antigone's fate: the original edict decreed death by stoning, but at one point he is going to have her executed publicly in front of Haemon; finally he opts for entombing her alive, but eventually revokes even this decision. He is the perfect example of the type of tragic character Aristotle described as 'consistently inconsistent' (*Poetics*, ch. 15).

Thinkers contemporary with Sophocles were involved in

the development of a political theory to match the needs of the new Athenian democracy. One concept being developed was that of *homonoia* or 'like-mindedness', according to which laws are ideally the results of a consensual or con-

---

POLITICAL JUSTICE IN A GREEK CITY-STATE

This excerpt from Hellas, *by the late and noted classical historian C.E. Robinson, describes a Greek city-state, or polis, as a political unit in which justice is dispensed by the will of the people.*

New ideas demand a new usage of words; and it is highly significant that "Polis" the Greek word for "city" was henceforth used for the "state." From the word is derived, of course, our own word "politics." And, more important, from the new synthesis of meaning was to spring our own conception of the State. That conception was not to be found in the previous civilizations of antiquity. No "politics" in our sense were possible under the absolute monarchs of Egypt or Mesopotamia. No genuine idea of "citizenship" is traceable among the Old Testament Jews. Their kings sent men to death like irresponsible despots; and when the Hebrew prophet denounced social wrongs, he appealed to the justice of Jehovah, not to the Rights of Man. It was not, in fact, until the Greek experiment was made that the whole life of a scattered populace was thus knit together in a constitutional system—a system which was at once the guarantee of the individual's civic liberties and also the focus of his civic loyalties and obligations.

Whoever said that men first came together in cities to find Justice, was not wide of the mark. . . . The Polis Justice [was] still more jealously guarded. The aristocratic judges would be more closely watched; and a stronger public opinion would be focussed on their decisions. Every citizen, rich or poor, well-born or commoner, was now legally on an equal footing. Fair play was to be the ever-growing demand of the masses; and there could be no worse outrage in the eyes of a true Greek than condemnation without proper trial. The privilege of arguing his case and standing up for his right was breath of life to him; and as a member of the Polis he was assured of that privilege. Justice, in short, was not least of the reasons why the new political union appealed to him, and why he came to take a conscious pride in his membership of the wider community.

C.E. Robinson, *Hellas: A Short History of Ancient Greece.* Boston: Beacon Press, 1955, pp. 28–29.

tractual agreement made by all the citizens of a state. Creon's law was passed autocratically, without *homonoia,* and his increasingly domineering attitude towards the views of others renders the disastrous outcome of his reign, and of the play, inevitable. As his own son puts it, 'The man | Who thinks that he alone is wise, that he | Is best in speech or counsel, such a man | Brought to the proof is found but emptiness.'

PUBLIC AND PRIVATE LIVES INTERTWINED

Creon is 'brought to the proof', however, not by civic disagreement articulated in the male arenas of council or assembly, but by a young female relative. This completely incenses him. Her goal is not political influence; she is simply obeying the divine law which laid on family members— especially women—the solemn duty of performing funeral rites for their kin. The mysterious, and often arrogant, Antigone is as inflexible as Creon is erratic; as the chorus comments, 'The daughter shows her father's temper— fierce, | Defiant; she will not yield to any storm.' It is Creon's misfortune that she happens to be not only Oedipus' daughter, but Creon's own niece and his son's fiancée. This calls the conventional dichotomy of public and private life into profound question; Creon cannot keep his two worlds separate, and the drama shows that they are as inextricably intertwined as the corpses of Antigone and Haemon, locked in a bizarre travesty of a nuptial embrace. If the play has a moral, it is that when political expediency cannot accommodate familial obligations and ritual observance of ancestral law, its advocates are courting disaster.

Respect for Community Is as Important as Respect for Loved Ones

Gilbert Norwood

In this excerpt from his book *Greek Tragedy*, the noted expert on ancient Greek drama Gilbert Norwood searches for the root cause of the terrible outcome of the confrontation between Antigone and Creon. Norwood concludes that the tragedy derives from the clash of two very different moral positions that have roughly equal value and importance in the society in which the story takes place.

The *Antigone* was produced about 441 B.C. The scene is laid before the palace at Thebes, on the morning after the repulse of the Argives who had come to restore Polynices. Creon, King of Thebes, publishes an edict that no one shall give burial to the corpse of Polynices on pain of death. Antigone, sister of the dead man, despite the advice of her sister Ismene, performs the rite and is haled before Creon. She insists that his edict cannot annul the unwritten primeval laws of Heaven. The king, disregarding the admonitions of his son Haemon, betrothed to Antigone, sends her to the cave of death. The prophet Tiresias warns him that the gods are angered by the pollution which comes from the unburied corpse. Urged by the chorus, Creon relents, and hastens first to bury Polynices, then to release Antigone, who has, however, already hanged herself. Haemon stabs himself by her body. On hearing of his death his mother Eurydice, wife of Creon, commits suicide. The play ends with Creon's helpless grief.

A TERRIBLE PROVOCATION

This play is perhaps the most admired of Sophocles' works. But the admiration often rests on a misunderstanding. It is

Excerpted from Gilbert Norwood, *Greek Tragedy* (New York: Hill and Wang, 1960).

customary to regard Antigone as a noble martyr and Creon
as a stupidly cruel tyrant, because of an assumption that she
must be what a similar figure would be, and often has been,
in a modern play. . . . The principle upheld by Antigone, and
that upheld by Creon, are . . . of equal validity. The poet may,
possibly, agree with Antigone rather than with the king, but
the current belief, that the princess is splendidly right and
her oppressor ignobly wrong, stultifies the play; it would become not tragedy but crude melodrama. In judging Attic
[Athenian] literature there is nothing which it is more vital
to remember than the immense importance attached by
Athenians to the State and its claims. We are alive to the
sanctity of human life, but think far less of the sanctity of national life. A [modern] reader, therefore, regards Creon with
all the reprobation which his treatment of Antigone can possibly deserve; but whatever justification is inherent in the
case he almost ignores.

The truth is that Creon commits a terrible act owing to a
terrible provocation. His act is the insult to Polynices' body,
which he maintains at the cost of Antigone's life; his justification is the fact that the dead man, though a Theban, was
attacking Thebes and would have destroyed the State.
Antigone stands for respect to private affection, Creon for respect to the community. It is impossible to say at the outset
which is the more important, and the problem may well be
insoluble. But it is precisely because of this that the *Antigone*
is a tragedy.

BOTH CHARACTERS ACT ON INSTINCT

To accept the customary view, and yet insist that Sophocles
is a great dramatist, is mere superstition; the work becomes
the record of an insane murder. . . . We may believe that
Sophocles by no means condemns Creon offhand. It is not
satisfactory to argue that Thebes should have been satisfied
with the death of the invader. Since he was a Theban his attack was looked on as the foulest treachery, which merited
extreme penalty, both by way of revenge and as a warning
to others. . . . The play presents a problem both for the king
and for his kinswoman: "I am right to punish this traitor's
corpse; am I justified in killing others who thwart the punishment?" "I am right to show love and pity for my dead
brother; am I justified in flouting the State?" Antigone is
only Creon over again with a different equipment of sympa-

thies. That one loves his country with a cold concentration which finds enemies and treachery everywhere, while the other passionately loves her dead brother, should not blind us to the truth that Antigone has all Creon's hardness and narrowness, and especially all his obstinacy. That tenderness and womanly affection which we attribute to the princess are amiable inventions of our own, except the love which she bears Polynices. This love is not to be in any sense belittled, but it is simply an instinct, like that of in matters of State, an instinct to which she will, like him, sacrifice all else. If Creon sacrifices Antigone for his ideal, she sacrifices Haemon for hers. He shows brutality to his son, she to her sister. That a compromise between the demands of the State and private conscience is, however unwelcome, necessary, never occurs to either party, and those who, like Haemon and Ismene, urge such a thought upon them are insulted.

DEPICTING AN ILLOGICAL PERSON

This blindness to the psychology of Antigone has led to actual meddling with Sophocles' text. In her last long speech occurs a celebrated "difficulty," namely, her statement that if the dead man had been a child or husband of hers, she would not thus have given her life; but the case of Polynices is different, since (her father and mother being dead) she can never have another brother. These lines are generally bracketed as spurious because unworthy of Antigone's character and inconsistent with the reason for her act which she has already given, namely, the "unwritten and unshaken laws of Heaven". Any idea that the passage was inserted in "later times" is rendered impossible by the fact that Aristotle quotes it (about 340 B.C.) and the presumption is that the words are the poet's own. Indeed, the "difficulty" exists only in the minds of those who attribute inconsistency in a character to incompetence in the playwright. But while illogical people exist it is hard to see why a dramatist should not depict them. Antigone's "reason" is stupid, no doubt, but what could be more dramatic? It is no novelty that a person capable of courageous action cannot argue well about it; there is a logic of the heart that has little to do with the logic of the brain. Antigone *has* no reasons; she has only an instinct. Here, and here only, Sophocles has pressed this point home, and the popular view has no resource but to reject the passage.

ANTIGONE'S SPLENDID BUT PERVERSE VALOUR

Whom does Sophocles himself approve, the king or his opponent? Neither. Attention to the plot will make this clear. The *peripeteia* or "recoil" is the revelation that the gods are angered by the pollution arising from the body, and that owing to their anger grave peril threatens Creon's family. It is this news which causes his change of purpose. Polynices is therefore buried by the king himself despite his edict. These facts show that ultimately both Antigone and Creon are wrong. Heaven is against Creon, as he is forced at last to see—Antigone's appeal to the everlasting unwritten laws is in this sense justified. But Antigone is wrong also. She should have left the gods to vindicate their own law. Such a statement may seem ignobly oblivious of religion, human nature, and the courage which she shows. But it is not denied that Antigone is noble and valiant: she may be both, yet mistaken and wrong-headed. One is bound to consider the facts of the plot. Why is she at first undetected yet compelled by circumstances to perform the "burial"-rites twice? Simply to remind us that, if Creon is resolved, she *cannot* "bury" Polynices. The king has posted guards, who remove the pious dust which she has scattered; and this gruesome contest could continue indefinitely. She throws away her life, *and with no possible confidence that her brother will in the end be buried.* It is precisely this blindness of hers which makes the tragedy—her union of noble courage and unswerving affection with inability to see the crude facts of a hateful situation. Her obstinacy brings about the punishment of Creon's obstinacy, for Eurydice's death is caused by Haemon's, and Haemon's by Antigone's. Had she not intervened all these lives would have been saved. The whole action might have dwindled to a mere revolting incident: the king's barbarity, the anger of the gods, and the king's submission. The tragedy would have disappeared: it is Antigone's splendid though perverse valour which creates the drama.

THE STATE IS MORE IMPORTANT THAN ONE PERSON

A difficulty of structure has been found in the fact that Creon, despite his haste to free Antigone, tarries for the obsequies [funeral rites] of Polynices. Why does he not save the living first? This "problem" arises merely from our insistence on the overwhelming importance of Antigone and our disregard of the real perspective. The explanation is simply that Creon has just been warned of the grave danger to the whole State and his family from the anger with which the gods view his treatment of Polynices—an offence which Tiresias emphasizes far more than that against Antigone; and the community, nay, even the several persons of Creon's family, are more important than one woman.

The lyrics of this play are among the finest in existence. The first ode expressing the relief of Thebes at the destruction of the ravening monster of war, the third which describes the persistence of sorrow from generation to generation of the Theban princes, the brief song which celebrates the all-compelling influence of love ... the last lyric, a graceful invocation to the God Dionysus, and above all, the famous ode upon man and his quenchless enterprise, all these are truly Attic in their serene, somewhat frigid, loveliness.

The Community Stands or Falls on the Rule of Law

C.M. Bowra

The ancient Greeks prided themselves in making laws to govern their communities and abiding by them. In this insightful tract, C.M. Bowra, renowned classical scholar and former vice chancellor of Oxford University, discusses how ordinary Greek men probably felt about a person, especially a woman, who willfully defied the law. In Sophocles' *Antigone*, Bowra points out, such men are represented by the chorus of Theban elders. They recite the now famous hymn of praise, the "ode to man" (i.e., humanity), stating that he and his community will remain strong as long as he obeys the law.

Antigone takes upon herself to defy the law or what is at least believed to be the law. The decision is momentous and would undoubtedly create strong prejudice against her in many of the audience. The Greeks, whose political liberties were intimately associated with the existence of laws, prided themselves upon them, with reason. It was the possession of laws that distinguished Greece from barbarian countries. . . . Antigone, in defiance of . . . this established sentiment, sets herself above Creon's law and claims to know better what is right. This is dangerous in anyone, and especially dangerous in a woman. At the outset of the play Antigone shows her contempt and hardly even troubles to explain it. It is not till she is confronted with Creon that she gives her reasons. In the interval she may well be suspected by a law-loving audience and condemned, if not for pride, at least for folly. Her determination to defy the laws requires considerable excuse. Sophocles was fully conscious of this. He knew how grave a

---

Excerpted from C.M. Bowra, *Sophoclean Tragedy* (Oxford: Oxford University Press, 1944). Reprinted by permission of Oxford University Press.

step Antigone takes and what will be thought of it. Only when the strength of the opposition has been revealed do we see how right Antigone is.

The qualms and misgivings that an ordinary man might feel about Antigone are dramatized in the Chorus. They are Theban elders whose natural instinct is to support the established power of Creon. In their first song they tell of their relief at the defeat and departure of the invaders. After such a strain they want nothing but peace and quiet, to forget the war. They are naturally averse to anyone who, like Antigone, seems likely to cause new troubles. But they have a certain decency and sense of honour, and are in fact typical citizens. They admit Creon's power to make what rules he pleases, but they do not say that they approve, and they claim that they are too old to see that his edict is carried out. They are uneasy about the refusal of burial to Polynices but not prepared to do anything about it. Still, when they hear of the first rites done to him, they are pleased and suggest that it may be the work of the gods. As Creon's tyrannical temper grows, they still offer little suggestions, say that Haemon has spoken well, and plead with success for the life of Ismene. They are perhaps not quite easy in their minds about what has happened. They accept Creon's edict for the sake of peace and quiet, but they are not convinced that it is right. For a time their desire for peace triumphs, and they condemn Antigone who disturbs it. Their position is hardly reasoned, but it is perfectly intelligible.

THE STRANGENESS OF HUMAN NATURE

The Chorus are able to consider the nature of Antigone's action without knowing that it is she who has committed it. Their first judgement is therefore impartial in so far as it is impersonal. In the song, [lines] 332–75, they give their general views on what the Guard has just reported and bring the burial of Polynices into its universal relations as they see them. This famous song on man is so often taken out of its context that its special dramatic relevance is obscured. It is not a hymn of praise to man's power, but something more complex and more closely related to the play. Behind it we may detect a song from Aeschylus' *Libation-Bearers* which begins, as this does, by stressing the strangeness of life:

Many strange dreads and griefs
Are the earth's fosterlings,

and goes on to tell of bold and criminal deeds attempted by women. The Chorus of the *Antigone* seem to follow this in a mood of surprise that anyone should dare to do what Antigone has just done in breaking Creon's edict. This action prompts them to consider man's strange paradoxical nature, which is composed of opposites and capable of great evil as of great good. In their shock and amazement they try to relate what has happened to what is almost a philosophy of history, to explain their disapproval by general principles, and at the same time to justify these principles. Their doctrine . . . is that the undeniable progress of man, his success in many spheres, his conquest of physical nature, and his establishment of an ordered society, are maintained and secured by the existence of laws. [The early Greek philosopher] Protagoras, according to Plato, described the advance of mankind in such terms, and at the end of his myth tells how [the head god] Zeus sends [the messenger god] Hermes to give men justice and decency, and orders him, 'And give a law from me, to kill as a disease in the city the man who cannot partake of decency and justice.'

THE MENACE OF ANARCHY

The root of this theory is that men are sustained and improved by law, and civilization rests on respect for it, because law brings with it the moral virtues. It is a noble and impressive theory, and the Chorus hold it. It is the climax and point of their song. The first three parts are concerned with the greatness of human achievements, but they are only a preliminary to the fourth part, which explains how laws and the respect for them make this achievement possible.

The essence of the song is its emphatic conclusion:

> With cunning beyond belief
> In subtle inventions of art
> He goes his way now to evil, now to good.
> When he keeps the laws of the land
> And the gods' rule he has sworn to hold,
> High is his city. No city has he
> Who in rash effrontery
> Makes wrongdoing his fellow.

From the variety of man's achievements the Chorus advance to the conclusion that he is capable of both evil and good, and that if he keeps the laws, all is well with him and his city, but if not, the city and he are ruined. The doctrine is plain. It is what Pericles, Protagoras, and Socrates believed about the laws—that they hold a city together, and that if they are broken, the individual is ruined no less than the city. Man is 'strange' because he has in himself such possibilities for good and for bad, for order and for destruction. The only real safeguard against his vagaries is the rule of laws which are, as Protagoras said, sanctioned by divine approval. If a man keeps them, the city stands; if he breaks them, he destroys its structure. The chief danger is presumptuous boldness, which was well known to be capable of destroying a city. After its great preliminaries and praise of man the song ends on a note of anxiety, a prayer that lawlessness may not prevail. The Chorus, anxious at all costs to keep order, are frightened by the menace of anarchy which the burial of Polynices seems to indicate.

This theory must have a particular reference and be concerned with something that has happened in the play. It cannot refer to Creon. He may have broken the laws of the gods, but these are not in question, and he certainly has not broken the laws of the land, which are. The Chorus refer to the yet unidentified person who, despite a legal order, has buried Polynices. They take their stand with Creon and, as they believe, with law and order. In fact they even echo his sentiments. When they say that obedience to the laws exalts a city, they repeat what he has said about the place of discipline in the State; their attack on rash boldness repeats his disapproval of those who are enemies of the city. In effect they condemn Antigone, though they do not know that she is the culprit. Nor is this surprising. The Chorus desire quiet. They will have nothing to do with law-breakers:

> May he never share my hearth,
> Never think thoughts of mine,
> Who does this.

Their feelings are quite understandable. Their song would appeal to a large number who felt that it was in any circumstances wrong to break the laws and that anyone who did so was presumptuous and wicked. The song expresses in advance a strong disapproval of Antigone and gives reasons for it.

The Chorus do not change their minds when they know who the criminal is. Despite their amazement that Antigone should have acted like this, they say

> What is this? Is it you who have disobeyed
> The laws of the king and are dragged hither,

Arrested in folly?

The emphatic mention of the laws after the importance given to them in the preceding song shows that the Chorus are still thinking on the same lines; Antigone has broken the laws, and the only explanation is that she has acted in senseless folly. To this view they hold with some obstinacy. Even when Antigone has made her great defence to Creon and shown that she does not recognize any validity in his so-called laws, the Chorus are not moved but comment:

> The father's cruel temper in the child
> Shows, and she knows not how to yield to trouble.

They see in her a pride closely akin to folly. Creon agrees with them and proceeds to dilate on the dangers of obstinacy. In what follows they take no part except to express surprise at Creon's decision that Haemon shall not marry Antigone and unwilling resignation when she is condemned to death. In effect they think that her action is wrong but that she is more foolish than wicked, and that she is punished with undue severity. They do not appreciate her real motives or the importance of what she has done.

THE CURSE OF OEDIPUS

In their next song, [lines] 582–625, the Chorus again expound their views of Antigone. If their earlier song was inspired by civic respect for law, this is inspired by considerations of moral theology. Protagoras gives place to [Sophocles' playwright colleague] Aeschylus. The song is an exposition in the Aeschylean manner of the hereditary evils of the House of Labdacus. In his *Seven against Thebes* Aeschylus had explained the misfortunes of Oedipus and his children by the belief that the gods punish the descendants of Laius to the third generation because he disobeyed an oracle. Sophocles may well have had his play in mind, since his Chorus, like that of Aeschylus, compare the successive waves of the curse to a stormy sea and see the human actors as victims of madness. Four times the Chorus refer to 'doom,' and it provides the main theme of their song. The gods have sent destruction on the family, and it is still potent. The Chorus believe that it is now at work on Antigone:

> Now over the last stock
> A light had been shed in Oedipus' house.
> But it is brought down

By the bloody dust of the nether gods,
Folly of words, and the heart's fury.

Antigone is the last of the house of Oedipus. All seemed well
with her until the handful of blood-stained dust which she
threw on Polynices became the instrument of her destruction. Her fault is a kind of madness, an hereditary fury that
works in her heart and drives her on as it drove on her father and grandfather before her.

The Chorus say about Antigone what Aeschylus might
have said. To some of the audience this might seem the right
view. It does not make her guilty of more than rash action
and bold speech; it explains her conduct and its punishment
by the wrath of the gods against her family and so excuses
her from any grave guilt herself. For those who felt it unjust
that Antigone should suffer as she does, such an explanation
might contain comfort. At least her suffering is not seen as a
monstrous act of injustice. We learn later that this is not the
poet's own view, but for the moment the Chorus produce a
theory which is reasonably tenable. . . . It sounds convincing. Actually it seems never to have been held by Sophocles,
who found other and different explanations of human suffering. Yet the power which he gives to its presentation
shows that he understood its appeal to many hearts. It was
one way of looking at a difficult moral problem, but it was
not the right way. Antigone does not act in folly and blindness of soul but from a clear knowledge of the divine will.
Such is human ignorance that it may mistake this for an almost criminal infatuation.

From their special account of Antigone's doom the Chorus
advance to more general considerations, especially to a noble address to Zeus, whose power no man can control:

To thy power, o Zeus,
What human trespass can fix bounds?

Against the illusions of men they set the everlasting, unsleep-
ing strength of Zeus, and give as an example one of his laws:

In what shall be and is to come,
In what was before, this law
Shall hold: nothing that grows too vast
Comes to men's life without a curse.

Their meaning is clear. This is their answer to Antigone's
claim that she is simply carrying out the gods' command.
Against the laws which she invokes they set up another, the
divine rule that men are victims of a doom or curse which

makes them think right what is wrong. They try to convict
her by her own methods, to turn the tables on her. She is
made to appear the victim of an illusion that she knows
what the gods' will really is. Once again Sophocles contrasts
her with Creon, who is really the victim of such an illusion.
The Chorus too are wrong, and they show it when against
Antigone's alleged foolishness they set up their own pretended wisdom.

The Chorus explain and condemn Antigone's action. They
persist in their view even when she appears for the last time
on her way to her living tomb. When they say to her,

> To uttermost effrontery
> You went, and with your steps you struck
> On Justice's high throne, my child:
> You are paying for your father's trespass,

they are still thinking in Aeschylean terms. They assume that
Antigone is guilty of criminal boldness and has attacked that
Justice which is embodied in the laws. They now see her as
a lawless spirit who attacks holy things and is doomed to disaster. The notion is familiar and needs little explanation.
Then, a little later, they seem to have changed their ground
and to be on the point of making some concession:

> All reverence should be revered,
> But power, to whomso power belongs,
> Must never be transgressed in aught.
> Your self-willed temper has destroyed you.

They admit after all that the honour in which she holds her
dead brother is a kind of reverence, but they try to compromise and to set against this the indubitable fact that authority will not brook disobedience. They seem to think that
Antigone's error lies in being one-sided, that she does not
fully understand the true meaning of reverence and of what
should be revered. They still think that her high temper has
ruined her. To the last fatal moment the Chorus maintain
their position with eloquence and power. For this the poet
must have had a good reason. Surely it is that he felt the
paradox of Antigone's action, knew the great honour in
which the laws of men are normally and rightly held, and
yet knew that she was right to resist them. To show the
forces against which she contends and the opposition that
any action like hers is bound to meet he makes the Chorus
condemn her on grounds which are at least specious and
would appeal to many in his audience.

CHAPTER 2

Antigone's Qualities and Motivations

READINGS ON
ANTIGONE

Love Is the Source of Antigone's Heroic Spirit

Bernard M.W. Knox

Throughout most of the play, Antigone staunchly maintains her moral stance about her right to bury her brother's body, regardless of Creon's order forbidding it. In her last scene, however, Bernard M.W. Knox suggests here, she sets aside her moral arguments and concentrates on the major event at hand, namely her own death. According to Knox, one of the twentieth century's premier classical scholars and translators, she will, in her mind, soon confront her dead relatives. She already sees herself as dead to the world of the living, he contends, and therefore shuts it out, showing that a deep love for her kin has been her guiding force all along.

The conflict between two individuals [in Sophocles' *Antigone*] represents the conflict between two different complexes of social and religious loyalties, one expressing the mood of the past, the other of the present. But we are never made to feel that these programs dominate the play, that Creon and Antigone are merely spokesmen of opposing ideologies. The formulation of their different points of view is a gradual development through the swift-moving action of the first half of the play; each new partial revelation of their fundamental beliefs is provoked by dramatic circumstance and action, and appears always as the natural expression of character. And in the second half of the play an astonishing thing happens. Both Antigone and Creon, as the pressure on them becomes intolerable, contradict and renounce the general principles they have claimed as support for their actions. The defense of their position falls back on purely personal considerations, unrelated to family, city, gods. "These people," said Haemon, speaking of the heroic temper, "when they are laid open . . .". . . . Both

Excerpted from Bernard M.W. Knox, *Heroic Temper: Studies in Sophoclean Tragedy.* Copyright ©1964 The Regents of the University of California. Reprinted by permission of the University of California Press.

of the antagonists . . . are laid open for us to see, and there is nothing there but the stubborn, individual, private will.

LOOKING DEATH IN THE FACE

For Antigone this surprising development is brought on suddenly by the immediate prospect of death. She made light of death before, welcomed it as a gain, claimed it as her choice, but now she is face to face with it, alone. "Even the bold," says Creon, "run away, when they see the death of their life near." Antigone does not weaken, but her mood does change. Before Creon she defiantly proclaimed her right and principle, but now she can think only of herself. She sings her own funeral lament. It is rudely interrupted by Creon, who orders his guards to take her away to her place of punishment. Her time has come; she is looking death in the face. There is no point now in explaining or defending her action to Creon or the chorus, and indeed she does not, in the famous speech which follows, address them at all. She speaks to her tomb, to her mother, to her brothers, first Eteocles, then Polynices. Her speech is addressed to the dead of her own family. She has performed the funeral rites for all of them, she says, last of all for Polynices, and for this her reward is death. So far she displayed the same complete loyalty to blood relationship and the rites of death she has championed all along, but at this point she makes a strange statement. "I would not, if I had been the mother of children, nor if my husband, dead, lay rotting in death, have taken this task on myself in defiance of my fellow citizens. In observance of what law do I say this? As for a husband, if he died, there could have been another, and another child from another man if I lost the first. But with my mother and father hidden in the realm of Hades, no brother could be born for me."

A CORRUPTED TEXT?

This speech is of course one of the most discussed in all Attic [Athenian] drama. . . . The argument has continued between those [scholars] who find the lines intolerable and those who, most of them with various degrees of misgiving, defend the text. Opinions are still as divided as ever, and no conclusive proofs are likely to be forthcoming; every reader must make up his own mind. It must however never be forgotten that to attack the authenticity of the passage is in this instance an especially radical piece of surgery, almost a counsel of despair. For the offending lines were in the text Aristotle read approximately a century after the first performance of the play, which means that our authority for this passage is better than what we have for most of the rest of the play—a manuscript written *fifteen* centuries after the performance. Not only that, but the casual manner in which Aristotle refers to the lines suggests strongly that in his time it was a celebrated passage, one everybody knew. If we are to believe that these lines were in fact inserted after Sophocles' death by some later actor, producer, or editor, we must face the consequences. And they are grave. Aristotle, the greatest scientific and scholarly intellect of the century after Sophocles, the most influential literary critic there has ever been, the head of a research school which busied itself among many other things with the history of tragedy, saw clearly the difficulties posed by the speech, and called the sentiment 'improbable' and so demanding an explanation by the poet, but it never for a moment occurred to him that the lines might be an interpolation. If they are, then we are forced to conclude that already, in Aristotle's time, the text of the *Antigone* was so fundamentally corrupt in a crucial passage that there was no criterion, no record, no tradition by which it could be corrected. Such a supposition deals a mortal blow to our confidence in the general soundness of the tragic texts. If that is possible, anything is, and we cannot object to those who would delete and transpose right and left. . . .

ALONE WITH THE DEAD

On the other hand it is no use closing our eyes to the difficulties the speech presents. [The renowned scholar-translator Sir Richard] Jebb, who condemns it, states the case against it most eloquently. "Her feet slip from the rock on which they were set; she suddenly gives up that which, throughout the drama, has been the immoveable basis of her action—the universal and unqualified validity of the divine law." There can be no doubt that she does exactly that; Hades desires the burial of a husband and a child just as much as that of a brother. She has for the moment ceased to speak as the champion of the gods below. Only for the moment, for in her very last speech as she is led off to her tomb she reasserts her claim. "See what I suffer . . . for my reverent observance of reverence." This fact has been used (by Jebb for example) against the authenticity of the speech in which her loyalty to the nether gods is abjured, but it serves rather to define the nature and suggest an explanation of that speech. In this final assertion of loyalty to the gods of death, as in all the others, she is addressing her fellow citizens and her enemy; she is making a claim, a defense, a protest. In the tortured speech in which she speaks so strangely she is talking neither to Creon nor to the chorus, but to the dead of her family, whom she is shortly to join. She is alone with them, oblivious of the presence of others; not one line in the speech is addressed to those present on stage. Like Ajax [the title character of another great Sophoclean play] in his great speech of agonized self-questioning, she struggles with her own emotions in a self-absorbed passion which totally ignores the presence of those around her.

THE GODS HAVE FAILED HER

This is the moment when in the face of death nothing matters but the truth. She is not trying to justify her action to others, she is trying to understand it herself. In the loneliness of her last moments in the sunlight, all that was secondary in her motives, all that was public rather than private, all that was self-comfort and hope, dissolves before her eyes, now made keen-sighted by the imminence of death. And one thing is very clear. The gods she championed have failed her. She says so herself: "Why should I in my misery look to the gods any more? Which of them can I call my ally?" A Christian martyr, secure in his faith and remembering that Christ rebuked those who demanded a 'sign' as a 'wicked and adulterous generation,' does not expect a miracle to save him or even a lesser manifestation of God's support. But the ancient Greek did. The world was full of signs and portents, omens and miracles: when Odysseus [the hero of Homer's epic poem *The Odyssey*] girds himself for the battle with the suitors he asks not for one sign of heaven's support, but two—one inside the house and one outside. And both are immediately sent.

ENTOMBED IN THE LAND OF THE LIVING

But Antigone is given no sign of approval or support, and though she will later in her last appeal to the chorus describe herself once again as the champion of reverence for the gods, she cannot offer herself that comfort now. She is reduced to purely human feelings; all that is left her is the love she bears the dead of her own blood. As she goes to join them she tells over her claims to their love and gratitude. She has performed the burial rites for all of them, last of all for Polynices, an action which has cost her her life. For him she has sacrificed her life as a woman—the husband and children she might have had. In the almost hysterical hyperbole of her claim that she would not have run such a risk for that husband and those children she will now never live to see, she is telling Polynices that no other love, not even that she might have had for the child of her own body, could surpass her love for him. The illogicality of her explanation cannot be denied. Her words—"with both parents dead, no other brother could be born"—are better grounds for saving a live brother than burying a dead one, and of course in the . . . passage Sophocles is adapting it *was* said of a live brother. But the illogicality can be understood; for Antigone the distinction between living and dead has ceased to exist. She has for some time now regarded herself as dead and she talks to Polynices as if he were alive; she is dead and about to be entombed in the land of the living, he is alive in the world of the dead.

She has abandoned her claim to be the champion of the nether gods, and, also, by her statement that she would not have risked as much for her own child, her position as champion of the blood relationship. In her moment of truth she is moved by nothing but her love for her dead family, not the family as an institution, a principle, but those individual human beings, father, mother, brothers, whom she now goes to join forever. The source of her heroic spirit is revealed, in the last analysis, as purely personal.

Antigone Dies for Her Principles

Bernard M.W. Knox

In this insightful essay, noted classical scholar
Bernard M.W. Knox argues that although at
the play's end it appears that Antigone has abandoned her principles, in fact she has not. She
seems mesmerized, he states, by the stark reality
of oncoming death, as if she is irresistibly drawn
to the world of the dead. Yet her final words reveal
that she remains steadfast in her reverence for and
advocacy of divine law (which expects humans
to bury their dead), the consistent basis of her
argument with Creon.

Antigone . . . is just as indifferent to Creon's principles of action as he is to hers. She mentions the city only in her last
agonized laments before she is led off to her living death:

> O my city, all your fine rich sons!
> . . . springs of the Dirce,
> holy grove of Thebes . . .   (934–36)

But here she is appealing for sympathy to the city over the
heads of the chorus, the city's symbolic representative on
stage. In all her arguments with Creon and Ismene she
speaks as one wholly unconscious of the rights and duties
membership in the city confers and imposes, as if no unit
larger than the family existed. It is a position just as extreme
as Creon's insistence that the demands of the city take precedence over all others, for the living and the dead alike.

IN THE NAME OF HADES

Like Creon, she acts in the name of gods, but they are different gods. There is more than a little truth in Creon's
mocking comment that Hades is "the one god she worships."
She is from the beginning "much possessed by death"; to-

gether with Ismene she is the last survivor of a doomed family, burdened with such sorrow that she finds life hardly worth living. "Who on earth," she says to Creon, "alive in the midst of so much grief as I, / could fail to find his death a rich reward?" She has performed the funeral rites for mother, father and her brother Eteocles:

> I washed you with my hands,
> I dressed you all, I poured the sacred cups
> across your tombs.   (989–91)

She now sacrifices her life to perform a symbolic burial, a handful of dust sprinkled on the corpse, for Polynices, the brother left to rot on the battlefield. She looks forward to her reunion with her beloved dead in that dark kingdom where Persephone, the bride of Hades, welcomes the ghosts. It is in the name of Hades, one of the three great gods who rule the universe, that she defends the right of Polynices and of all human beings to proper burial. "Death [Hades] longs for the same rites for all," she tells Creon—for patriot and traitor alike; she rejects Ismene's plea to be allowed to share her fate with an appeal to the same stern authority: "Who did the work? / Let the dead and the god of death bear witness!" In Creon's gods, the city's patrons and defenders, she shows no interest at all. Zeus she mentions twice: once as the source of all the calamities that have fallen and are still to fall on the house of Oedipus and once again at the beginning of her famous speech about the unwritten laws. But the context here suggests strongly that she is thinking about Zeus in his special relationship to the underworld, Zeus *Chthonios* (Underworld Zeus). "It wasn't Zeus," she says,

> who made this proclamation. . . .
> Nor did that Justice, dwelling with the gods
> beneath the earth, ordain such laws for men.   (499–502)

From first to last her religious devotion and duty are to the divine powers of the world below, the masters of that world where lie her family dead, to which she herself, reluctant but fascinated, is irresistibly drawn.

A SPECTACULAR BETRAYAL

But, like Creon, she ends by denying the great sanctions she invoked to justify her action. In his case the process was spread out over the course of several scenes, as he reacted to each fresh pressure that was brought to bear on him; Antigone turns her back on the claims of blood relationship and the nether gods in one sentence: three lines in Greek, no more. They are the emotional high point of the speech she makes just before she is led off to her death.

> Never, I tell you,
> if I had been the mother of children
> or if my husband died, exposed and rotting—
> I'd never have taken this ordeal upon myself,
> never defied our people's will.   (995–99)

These unexpected words are part of the long speech that concludes a scene of lyric lamentation and is in effect her farewell to the land of the living. They are certainly a total

---

A PERSIAN WIFE CHOOSES HER BROTHER OVER HER SONS

This is the passage from Herodotus's Histories *that inspired the speech in which Antigone states she would choose to save her brother before her husband or children.*

He [Darius, the Persian king] had him [Intaphrenes, a Persian noble accused of treason] arrested with his children and all his near relations, in the strong suspicion that he and his family were about to raise a revolt. All the prisoners were then chained, as condemned criminals. After his arrest, Intaphrenes' wife came to the palace and began to weep and lament outside the door, and continued so long to do so that Darius, moved to pity by her incessant tears, sent someone out to speak to her. 'Lady,' the message ran, 'the king is willing to spare the life of one member of your family—choose which of the prisoners you wish to save.' Having thought this offer over, the woman answered that, if the king granted her the life of one only of her family, she would choose her brother. The answer surprised Darius, and he sent again and asked why it was that she rejected her husband and children, and preferred to save her brother, who was neither so near to her as her children, nor so dear as her husband. 'My lord,' she replied, 'God willing, I may get another husband, and other children when these are gone. But as my father and mother are both dead, I can never possibly have another brother. That was the reason for what I said.' Darius appreciated the lady's good sense, and, to mark his pleasure, granted her not only the life she asked, but also that of her eldest son. The rest of the family were all put to death.

Herodotus, *The Histories*. Trans. Aubrey de Selincourt. New York: Penguin Books, 1972, p. 252.

repudiation of her proud claim that she acted as the champion of the unwritten laws and the infernal gods, for, as she herself told Creon, those laws and those gods have no preferences, they long "for the same rites for all." And her assertion that she would not have done for her children what she has done for Polynices is a spectacular betrayal of that fanatical loyalty to blood relationship which she urged on Ismene and defended against Creon, for there is no closer relationship imaginable than that between the mother and the children of her own body. Creon turned his back on his guiding principles step by step, in reaction to opposition based on those principles; Antigone's rejection of her public values is just as complete, but it is the sudden product of a lonely, brooding introspection, a last-minute assessment of her motives, on which the imminence of death confers a merciless clarity. She did it because Polynices was her brother; she would not have done it for husband or child. She goes on to justify this disturbing statement by an argument which is more disturbing still: husband and children, she says, could be replaced by others but, since her parents are dead, she could never have another brother. It so happens that we can identify the source of this strange piece of reasoning; it is a story in the *Histories* of Sophocles' friend Herodotus (a work from which Sophocles borrowed material more than once). Darius the Great King had condemned to death for treason a Persian noble, Intaphrenes, and all the men of his family. The wife of Intaphrenes begged importunately for their lives; offered one, she chose her brother's. When Darius asked her why, she replied in words that are unmistakably the original of Antigone's lines. But what makes sense in the story makes less in the play. The wife of Intaphrenes saves her brother's life, but Polynices is already dead; Antigone's phrase "no brother could ever spring to light again" would be fully appropriate only if Antigone had managed to save Polynices' life rather than bury his corpse. . . .

THE DEAD AGAINST THE STATE

This is Antigone's third and last appearance on stage; in the prologue she planned her action, in the confrontation with Creon she defended it, and now, under guard, she is on her way to the prison which is to be her tomb. In lyric meters, the dramatic medium for unbridled emotion, she appeals to the chorus for sympathy and mourns for the marriage hymn she will never hear (this is as close as she ever comes to mentioning Haemon). She gets little comfort from the Theban elders; the only consolation they offer is a reminder that she may be the victim of a family curse—"do you pay for your father's terrible ordeal?"—a suggestion that touches her to the quick and provokes a horror-struck rehearsal of the tormented loves and crimes of the house of Oedipus. There is, as she goes on to say, no one left to mourn her; the lyric lament she sings in this scene is her attempt to provide for herself that funeral dirge which her blood relatives would have wailed over her corpse, if they had not already preceded her into the realm of Hades. This is recognized by Creon, who cuts off the song with a sarcastic comment: "if a man could wail his own dirge *before* he dies, / he'd never finish." And he orders the guards to take her away.

Her song cut off, she turns from the lyric medium of emotion to spoken verse, the vehicle of reasoned statement, for her farewell speech. It is not directed at anyone on stage; it resembles a soliloquy, a private meditation. It is an attempt to understand the real reasons for the action that has brought her to the brink of death. After an address to the tomb and prison where she expects to be reunited with her family she speaks to Polynices (Creon is referred to in the third person). It is to Polynices that she is speaking when she says that she would not have given her life for anyone but a brother; it is as if she had already left the world of the living and joined that community of the family dead she speaks of with such love. Now, in the face of death, oblivious of the presence of Creon and the chorus, with no public case to make, no arguments to counter, she can at last identify the driving force behind her action, the private, irrational imperative which was at the root of her championship of the rights of family and the dead against the demands of the state. It is her fanatical devotion to one particular family, her own, the doomed, incestuous, accursed house of Oedipus and especially to its most unfortunate member, the brother whose corpse lay exposed to the birds and dogs. When she tells him that she has done for him what she would not have done for husband or children she is not speaking in wholly hypothetical terms, for in sober fact she has sacrificed, for his sake, her marriage to Haemon and the children that might have issued from it.

HER UNJUST FATE

And in this moment of self-discovery she realizes that she is absolutely alone, not only rejected by men but also abandoned by gods. "What law of the mighty gods have I transgressed?" she asks—as well she may, for whatever her motive may have been, her action was a blow struck for the rights of Hades and the dead. Unlike Christians whose master told them not to look for signs from heaven (Matthew 16:4), the ancient Greek expected if not direct intervention at least some manifestation of favor or support from his gods when he believed his cause was just—a flight of eagles, the bird of Zeus, or lightning and thunder, the signs which, in the last play, summon Oedipus to his resting place. But Antigone has to renounce this prospect: "Why look to the heavens any more . . . ?" She must go to her death as she has lived, alone, without a word of approval or a helping hand from men or gods. . . .

Before the raw immediacy of death . . . she has sounded the depths of her own soul and identified the determinant of those high principles she proclaimed in public. But that does not mean that they were a pretense, still less that she has now abandoned them. She dies for them. In her very last words, as she calls on the chorus to bear witness to her unjust fate, she claims once more and for the last time that she is the champion of divine law—she suffers "all for reverence, my reverence for the gods!"

By Acting Like a Man, Antigone Provokes Fear and Hostility

Sarah B. Pomeroy

Antigone lived in a male-dominated society in which women were expected to be submissive and obedient. But in defying Creon she takes on what are seen by her contemporaries as masculine traits; he reacts, predictably, with fear and suspicion. Sarah B. Pomeroy, professor of classics at Hunter College and the graduate school of the City University of New York, here proposes that in writing *Antigone* Sophocles consciously addressed the issue of gender. Although he accepted that men should run society, she suggests, he was concerned about placing too much value on male traits at the expense of female ones. And having Antigone assume a man's role forced men to examine their own hostility toward uppity women.

The portrayal of the masculine woman as heroine was fully developed in Sophocles' *Antigone*. The play opens with the daughters of Oedipus lamenting the laws established by the tyrant Creon. Their brother Polynices lies dead, but Creon has forbidden that the corpse be buried, as punishment for the dead man's treachery against his native land. While Antigone urges that they perform the burial rites, her sister Ismene seizes upon the excuse that they are not men: "We were born women, showing that we were not meant to fight with men." She uses the frequently significant verb *phyō*, implying that it is by nature (*physis*) rather than by manmade convention that women do not attempt to rival men.

FEARS IN A PATRIARCHAL SOCIETY

Creon, a domineering ruler, reveals particular hostility in his relations with the opposite sex. His prejudices are patri-

From *Goddesses, Wives, Whores, and Slaves*, by Sarah B. Pomeroy. Copyright ©1975 by Sarah B. Pomeroy. Adapted by permission of Schocken Books, distributed by Pantheon Books, a division of Random House, Inc. *The subheads have been added to this reprint.*

archal [part of a system dominated by a father figure]. He cannot understand his son Haemon's love for Antigone, but refers to a wife as a "field to plow.". . . Since the male seed is all-important, any female will suffice. . . . [Scholar] Simone de Beauvoir, in *The Second Sex,* traced the phallus/plow-woman/furrow as a common symbol of patriarchal author-ity and subjugation of woman. Moreover, as modern femi-nists have pointed out, the repressive male cannot conceive of an equal division of power between the sexes, but fears that women, if permitted, would be repressive in turn. So Creon, the domineering male, is constantly anxious about being bested by a woman and warns his son against such a humiliation.

On the other hand, Ismene—perhaps because she stayed at Thebes while Antigone shared the exile of her father—has been indoctrinated into the beliefs of patriarchal society: men are born to rule, and women to obey. Antigone bitterly rejects her sister's notion of the natural behavior of women. Polynices is buried secretly, and Creon, the guard, and the chorus all suppose that only a man could have been respon-sible. Thereupon forced to confess to Creon that she has in fact buried her brother, Antigone refers to herself with a pro-noun in the masculine gender. Creon, in turn, perceives her masculinity and refers to Antigone by a masculine pronoun. . . . He resolves to punish her, declaring, "I am not a man, she is the man if she shall have this success without penalty." (Similarly, [the fifth-century-B.C. Greek historian] Herodotus notes that Queen Artemisia, who participated in [Persian king] Xerxes' expedition against Greece, was con-sidered masculine, and that the Athenians were so indignant that a woman should be in arms against them that for her capture alone they offered a financial reward.)

A MASCULINE SORT OF WOMAN

Feeling, then, that in daring to flout his commands Antigone has acted as a man—for a true woman would be incapable of opposition—Creon, when he declares sentence upon the sisters, asserts that "they must now be women." However, he continues to refer to them in the masculine gender. The re-peated use of a masculine adjective to modify a feminine noun is noteworthy, because in classical Greek, adjectives regularly agree with the gender of the modified noun (the masculine gender may be used in reference to a woman when a general statement is made).

We may note the male orientation of the Greek language, in which general human truths, though conceived as referring specifically to women, can be cast in the masculine gender. Perhaps this grammatical explanation will suffice when the change in gender is sporadic. However, the masculine gender used to refer to a female in specific rather than general statements—a rare occurrence in Greek—occurs with significant frequency in *Antigone.* It is, I believe, a device used by the playwright in characterizing the heroine who has become a masculine sort of woman. In her penultimate [next to last] speech, Antigone explains her willingness to die for the sake of a brother, though not for a husband or child.

> For had I been a mother, or if my husband had died, I would never have taken on this task against the city's will. In view of what law do I say this? If my husband were dead I might find another, and another child from him if I lost a son. But with my mother and father hidden in the grave, no other brother could ever bloom for me.

Herodotus also relates a story about a woman who, when offered the life of a husband, a son, or a brother, chooses a brother for the same reason as Antigone.

THE PRECIOUS BROTHER-SISTER BOND

A number of Sophoclean scholars have judged the speech spurious [inauthentic, i.e., not written by Sophocles], or pronounced the sentiments unworthy of the heroine. They consider the choice of a brother over a child bizarre. And yet, in the context of Classical Athens, Antigone's choice is reasonable. Mothers could not have been as attached to children as the ideal mother is nowadays. The natural mortality of young children would seem to discourage the formation of strong mother-child bonds. In addition, patriarchal authority asserted that the child belonged to the father, not the mother. He decided whether a child should be reared, and he kept the child upon dissolution of a marriage, while the woman returned to the guardianship of her father or, if he were dead, her brother. Thus the brother-sister bond was very precious.

The preference for the brother is also characteristic of the masculine woman, who may reject the traditional role of wife and mother as a result of being inhibited by external forces from displaying cherishing or nurturing qualities. The masculine woman often allies herself with the male members of her family. In this context we may note Antigone's firm and repeated denunciations of her sister. She also judges her mother harshly, blaming her for the "reckless guilt of the marriage bed," while the chorus, seeing only her father's disposition in her, calls her "cruel child of a cruel father." Her disregard of her sister is so complete that she actually refers to herself as the sole survivor of the house of Oedipus.

In the end, Antigone reverts to a traditional female role. She laments that she dies a virgin, unwed and childless, and commits suicide after being entombed alive by Creon. In classical mythology, suicide is a feminine and somewhat cowardly mode of death.... Haemon ... kills himself for love, justifying Creon's earlier concern over his "womanish" tendencies. Of all tragic heroines, Antigone was the most capable of learning through suffering and achieving a tragic vision comparable to that of Oedipus [her father, who unknowingly killed his father and married his mother, and then blinded himself when he found out]. Her death erased that possibility.

The fate of Haemon illustrates the destructive quality of love. The chorus gives voice to this idea:

> Love, invincible love, who keeps vigil on the soft cheek of a young girl, you roam over the sea and among homes in wild places, no one can escape you, neither man nor god, and the one who has you is possessed by madness. You bend the minds of the just to wrong, so here you have stirred up this quarrel of son and father. The love-kindling light in the eyes of the fair bride conquers.

TRADITIONAL DISTINCTIONS BETWEEN THE SEXES

Antigone is a complex and puzzling play. According to Athenian law, Creon was Antigone's guardian, since he was her nearest male relative. As such, he was responsible for her crime in the eyes of the state, and his punishing her was both a private and public act. He was also the nearest male relative of his dead nephews, and he, not Antigone, was responsible for their burial. Creon put what he deemed to be the interests of the state before his personal obligations.

The differences between Creon and Antigone are traditional distinctions between the sexes. According to [the famed modern psychoanalyst Sigmund] Freud, "Women spread around them their conservative influence. . . . Women represent the interests of the family and sexual life; the work of civilization has become more and more men's business." The civilizing inventions of men are listed by the chorus of *Antigone:* sailing, navigation, plowing, hunting, fishing, domesticating animals, verbal communication, building houses, and the creation of laws and government. These were mainly masculine activities.

The Greeks assumed that men were bearers of culture. For example, according to myth, Cadmus brought the alphabet to Greece; Triptolemus—albeit prompted by the goddess Demeter—brought the use of the plow; while Daedalus was credited with the scissors, the saw, and other inventions. The specific achievements of women—which were probably in the realm of clothing manufacture, food preparation, gardening, and basketmaking, and the introduction of olive culture by [the goddess] Athena—do not appear in Sophocles' list. . . .

Creon's lack of insight into the necessity of the duality of male and female led to the death of Antigone and to his own annihilation as well. Creon's wife died cursing him. Moreover, in a society where sons were expected to display filial obedience, Haemon chose Antigone over his father and his choice was not held against him. His death was not a punishment for disobedience. *Antigone* and many other tragedies show the effect of overvaluation of the so-called masculine qualities (control, subjugation, culture, excessive cerebration) at the expense of the so-called feminine aspects of life (instinct, love, family ties) which destroys men like Creon. The ideal, we can only assume—since Sophocles formulates no solution—was a harmonization of masculine and feminine values, with the former controlling the latter.

Why Does Antigone Kill Herself?

Jan Kott

This perceptive and thought-provoking essay is by the noted literary scholar and critic Jan Kott. He addresses Antigone's suicide, pointing out that the version of the story written by the playwright's distinguished colleague Euripides (author of *Medea*) ends with Antigone surviving. Why, Kott wonders, does Sophocles' heroine choose to take her own life? Kott suggests that it is not fear of a long and drawn-out death in the cave that prompts her to kill herself, but rather her inability to deal with the hate and rejection of her community. Like respect for the dead, the acceptance, sympathy, and support of one's community is a fundamental need shared by people in all times and places.

She was so brave. And so fearless. She knew what was in store for her. She was fifteen, at most sixteen years old. And very tiny. The guards said that when she found the corpse exposed she cried like a bird finding its nest despoiled. Not strong enough to lift the body, she sprinkled it with 'thirsty dust' and poured over it wine from the pitcher she had brought with her. And no sooner had the guards once more swept away the earth from the corpse than she came back and repeated the ritual, although it had been publicly announced that the penalty for doing so was stoning to death.

BURIAL CUSTOMS VERY ANCIENT

A true daughter of Oedipus, she was as stubborn as her father. Oedipus had long since been banished from Thebes and was wandering throughout Greece loudly lamenting his fate. Even before that her mother Jocasta had hanged herself with her silken belt. Antigone was left with a younger sister

Reprinted from Jan Kott, "Why Did Antigone Kill Herself?" *New Theater Quarterly*, vol. 9, no. 34 (May 1993), pp. 107–109, by permission of the author. *Endnotes in the original have been omitted in this reprint.*

and two brothers. The younger brother had attacked Thebes with a foreign army; the elder defended the city. They joined in a duel to the death and both fell at the city's gates. Creon ordered that the defender of Thebes be given a funeral with full military honours; the traitor's body was to be left unburied, 'a feast for birds and scavenging dogs'.

But for Antigone the city's foe had not ceased to be her brother. She chose to defy the law. 'That final Justice', she said to Creon, 'that rules the world below makes no such law.' Antigone gave her brother the only burial possible under the circumstances: a symbolic burial. Even in our days the common custom is for the relatives and closest friends of the deceased to throw the first handfuls of earth on the coffin being lowered into the ground.

In his reflections on tragedy, [the early-nineteenth-century German philosopher Georg W.F.] Hegel says that the soldier belongs to the state. That is, as long as he is still alive. But when he dies, the body is returned to his family. In America where in many states the death penalty has been reinstituted, on the day after the execution, rendered humane by a lethal injection or the electric chair, the body of the condemned prisoner is returned to his family. During the night preceding the execution a candlelight vigil similar to a wake is often held in front of the prison walls. The next morning the relatives or the opponents of the death penalty accompany the wooden coffin. To the burial.

According to the archaic beliefs of which Babylonian hymns speak directly and whose traces are still to be found in Homer, the spirit of an unburied person must haunt the places which he had previously frequented in his earthly life and where he can never find peace. Belief in life after death has taken many forms, but burial or cremation of the dead goes back to the very beginnings of the human community. And after hundreds of thousands of years, burial sites are frequently the only evidence of past civilizations which have left no other traces.

VISITING THE DECEASED

To the Victorian readers of *Antigone* and its classic commentators, Creon's injunction against burying Polynices might have seemed far removed from anything they knew about or had experienced themselves. But for us who have lived through the greater part of the twentieth century, and especially its second and third quarters, Creon's decree and Antigone's drama seem quite ordinary. Ideologies have conferred upon the state, its philosophers, and its policemen power not only over the living but also over the dead, and not only as to their rank and place in history but also their right to a grave.

The most visible trace left behind by the dead, their final physical presence on the earth, is the grave. One visits the grave as though one were visiting the deceased. The lack of a grave for our friends and relatives, the absence of knowledge of where and when their bodies have been thrown, is one of the greatest wrongs done to those who have survived.

My father was taken to his death from the former St. Michael's prison in Cracow [in Poland] on the day he was supposed to have been released. I do not know where he was murdered or in what ditch his body was thrown. A son says the Kadish [a Jewish prayer or hymn] on the anniversary of his father's death. In synagogues the world over once a year the Kadish is said for all those about whom nothing is known as to where and when they were put into the ground or turned into ashes. After two thousand five hundred years Antigone's experience has once again become something familiar and tangible for many of us. And as painful as ever.

A MASTER OF RETARDATION

'For you chose to live when I chose death', Antigone says to Ismene, who was afraid to help her bury their brother. Antigone was ready for death, but for a death that would be inflicted on her by others, not for a death that she would inflict on herself. Why then did she kill herself? Among all the hundreds and even the thousands of those who have been waiting for seemingly certain death for long months or even years, hungry, constantly humiliated, and often tortured, only a handful have shortened the agony of waiting by taking their own lives. And it can never ultimately be known whether they had been 'coaxed' to do it. They certainly did not hurry in choosing death. Why then did Antigone act in such haste?

The defeat and death of the protagonist [main character] always seemed inevitable in tragedies from the Greeks to Shakespeare. . . . That was what is called tragic necessity. *Antigone* is perhaps the only exception to the rule, or at least the only one I know of. In *Antigone* the optimistic conclusion remains unrealized, but it seems almost palpable, hovering over the tragedy. If Antigone had not acted in such haste, if she had waited a little longer—a couple of minutes of theatrical time or a few hours more locked away on that fateful afternoon in that dark chamber in Thebes—before putting the noose around her neck, as her mother had done with her silken belt, Creon and his servants could have come in time to move the rock and set her free.

Sophocles is an unsurpassed master of retardation [delaying the climax to build suspense]. The tyrant is already frightened by Teiresias's prophecy and Creon is ready to bury Polynices with his own hands and free Antigone from the dark dungeon. But which should he do first and where should he go first? Sophocles leaves the decision to Creon and in so doing suspends for a moment the tragic resolution. Had Creon gone to the vault first, Antigone would not have put the rope around her neck and Haemon would not have struck at Creon with his sword before killing himself with it. And Creon's wife, Eurydice, would not have committed suicide. Euripides' tragedy about Antigone, of which almost nothing survives, ended with the marriage of Haemon and Antigone, the daughter of Oedipus. Thus Euripides' trilogy of Theban tragedies ended with a melodrama.

MUST AFFRONT BE THROWN IN MY FACE?

Why did Sophocles' Antigone kill herself? Greek tragedy does not use the psychological soliloquy, we know nothing of Antigone's thoughts in the dark cavern, and even if she had talked to herself, no one heard her voice. But the one thing we do know is her last experience as she was led under guard through the streets of Thebes to the dungeon. She was accompanied by the chorus of Theban elders. We know what the chorus said to that girl going to her death and we know what Antigone said to them in answer.

> Laughter against me now.
> In the name of our fathers' gods,
> could you not wait till I went?
> Must affront be thrown in my face?

The Theban elders reproached Antigone for nurturing in her heart the same rage as had her father Oedipus, and they laughed at her as impious when she dared compare herself to [the mythological character] Niobe, an equal of the gods turned into stone from grief.

Two or three years ago when I was in Budapest [in Hungary] I saw a production of a native renaissance passion play. On the Hungarian stage white robed and garlanded girls showered flowers on Jesus upon his entry into Jerusalem on White Sunday. Old men raised both their arms to the heavens in a gesture of greeting. But a moment later the same innocent virgins spat on Jesus and threw stones at him as the executioners led him away to his death. The Elders of Jerusalem covered their faces with their cloaks. Women giggled at the sight of Christ beaten and humiliated on his way to Calvary.

> Why, my friends, in the name
> of all our fathers' gods
>
> $\qquad\qquad\qquad\qquad$ do you mock me?
>
> Why can you not wait
>
> $\qquad\qquad\qquad\qquad$ till I am gone
>
> to hurl abuse at my face
>
> $\qquad\qquad\qquad\qquad$ O city
> $\qquad\qquad\qquad$ of lordly sons,
> $\qquad\qquad\qquad$ my noble Thebes!
> $\qquad\qquad$ Sweet springs of Dirke,
> sacred groves glorious for her chariots!
>
> $\qquad\qquad\qquad\qquad\qquad$ You!
> $\qquad\qquad\qquad\qquad\qquad$ You I call!
>
> Bear witness and remember
> as I walk to my rocky prison
> $\qquad\qquad\qquad$ unwept.
> Remember the unjust law
>
> $\qquad\qquad\qquad$ that sends me there
> $\qquad\qquad\qquad\qquad$ friendless.
> $\qquad\qquad$ Drowned in sorrow,
> alive, I have no home among the living;
> dead, I am an alien without rights.

These are almost Antigone's last words. She killed herself because she could not bear to live even a moment longer once she had been thrown into that dark dungeon. Victims arouse hate. Antigone could not survive hate.

CHAPTER 3

The Play's Other Characters

READINGS ON
ANTIGONE

A General Breakdown of the Characters

William N. Bates

This concise summary of the characters of Sophocles' *Antigone* serves as an expanded version of the
usual list of characters that appears at the beginning
of a play. It is excerpted from *Sophocles: Poet and
Dramatist*, a useful study of Sophocles' works by the
late William N. Bates, a former professor of Greek
language and literature at the University of Pennsyl-
vania. Bates also refers here to another of Sophocles'
great tragedies, *Oedipus Tyrannus* (*Oedipus the King*),
since some of the characters appear in both plays.

When one stops to consider the *dramatis personae* he finds
that the principal character is, as it should be, Antigone. She
dominates the play from the beginning, although a counting
of the lines shows that she is not on the stage as much of the
time as Creon. She is before the audience while 435 lines are
spoken, while Creon is present during 789. The play, according to the generally accepted text, contains 1,353 lines.
And yet one cannot imagine the play named for Creon.

ANTIGONE

There is nothing in the character of Antigone as the dramatist presents her which calls for profound psychological
analysis. It is, indeed, very simple. She is a sincere young girl
inspired by a lofty purpose which she conceives to be a
solemn duty. The idea that this duty is something which she
might, perhaps, avoid does not for a moment occur to her; nor
that she must avoid it to save her life. It is with her, as Aristotle says, a case of the universal law superior to the written
law. The penalty is a detail to which at the moment she gives
no serious thought. With this firmly fixed in her mind it is not
surprising that she cannot understand the attitude of her sis-

ter Ismene. But Sophocles has no intention of representing her as if she were a religious enthusiast bent on martyrdom, so that we should not be surprised at the reaction which comes to her after the deed is done. Many commentators have not understood this, especially where she says that she would not have done it for a husband or a son. But she has never had either. . . . The poet wants to show that Antigone is, in reality, not so very different from other people. It is as if she were thinking out loud. She is going over and over in her own mind all that has occurred. Life is as dear to her as to anyone, and she is convinced now that she never could have done what she did for any other than Polynices. This moment of weakness is surely natural, and the fact that the poet felt it to be so is evidence of his dramatic instinct. It does not detract from our interest in or our pity for her. She is a pathetic figure to the end, the most pathetic of all the characters of Sophocles, except Oedipus after his downfall. . . .

ISMENE

In direct contrast with Antigone is the character of Ismene. She is represented as a timid young girl with none of the resoluteness of purpose which her sister has, nor her high moral sense of duty. She is terrified by the king's edict and dares not aid her sister. Her feelings are well expressed in [the lines]:

> But this we must remember that we are
> Born women and not fit to fight with men.

And . . .

> Those in authority I shall obey.

Antigone cannot understand this attitude of mind and scorns it.

> I love not one who loves me just with words,

she says. But when Antigone's guilt has been established and she has been condemned, Ismene, though innocent, is ready to share in her punishment. Ismene may be of common clay, yet the poet does not wish us to imagine her as lacking in courage or in sisterly affection. The difference in character in the two daughters of Oedipus is, however, sharply drawn.

CREON AND HAEMON

The part of Creon calls for little comment. He is the villain in the play and is represented consistently. He is a man of small mind conscious of his weakness, but very jealous of his prerogatives. He is king and he is determined to seem a great man to all his people. His edict must be law regardless of all consequences. Such a character is not hard to understand. In his punishment of his enemies, of all in fact who oppose him, he is too severe, and this severity results in his own ruin. Creon is punished as it was right that he should be, and in the end utterly crushed. . . .

Haemon is a gentle youth whose love for Antigone is sincere. He wants to help her; but at the same time is overawed by the importance of his father's official position and by dread of him. When, near the end of the play, he rushes at Creon sword in hand and then turns the weapon against himself, it is the despair of a timid soul. Aristotle cites this as an example of a person about to do a dreadful deed knowingly and then refraining, a rather rare motive in tragedy which he condemns as untragic. Unusual, too, is the love motive. The character of Haemon is, however, as clearly drawn as is that of Antigone or Creon.

THE OTHER CHARACTERS

Of the remaining personages in the play, Tiresias is represented as in the *Oedipus Tyrannus.* He is the same blind seer whose powers are unquestioned by the Thebans and yet, with all his prophetic art, very irascible; and just as in the *Oedipus Tyrannus* he utters dreadful prophecies which turn out true. Tiresias is consistently represented in both plays.

Eurydice, the wife of Creon, has a short but striking part. She speaks but nine lines, listens intently to the report of the messenger and then departs without a word. This silent exit of the queen must have been very effective in the theatre. No speech which she could have uttered could have produced the same effect as this tragic silence. One could not find a better example of the dramatic skill of Sophocles. . . .

The guard is particularly well handled by the dramatist. He is a man of the lower class, upon whom has been laid an unpleasant and dangerous duty which he cannot avoid. He must tell the king that his edict has been defied and the culprit not detected. He is worried and tries to conceal his anxiety by treating the matter lightly. He thinks he can best save his own skin by playing the buffoon. All this is natural. Alongside of him we must place the shepherd of Laius in the *Oedipus Tyrannus.* Sophocles was particularly happy in depicting such characters.

There is little to say about the messengers other than that they tell the stories which they have to tell clearly, but without the vividness characteristic of messengers' speeches in Euripides. . . .

NO ROLE FOR A GREAT ACTOR?

The criticism may, perhaps, be made that the *Antigone* does not afford a great tragic actor a good opportunity to show his skill. This is true. There is no part in the play which can be compared with that of Oedipus in the *Oedipus Tyrannus*. The *Antigone* was not written with such an end in view. It depended for its success upon the way in which the incidents of the plot were presented. The play is good proof that a tragedy may be great without providing a rôle for a great actor. At the same time it is evident that the *Antigone* might be effectively presented even with actors of moderate ability, and no doubt that often happened.

The Mythical Sources of the Characters

Joan V. O'Brien

Most of the characters and stories in the plays of the great fifth-century-B.C. Greek dramatists Sophocles, Aeschylus, and Euripides were from popular myths. For instance, the incident in which two brothers fight for possession of Thebes, which Sophocles used in *Antigone* and Aeschylus in *Seven Against Thebes*, came from an old myth. The eighth-century-B.C. epic poet Homer, the somewhat later poet Hesiod, and the early fifth-century lyric poet Pindar all mentioned it in their writings. Thus, some of the characters in *Antigone* came from well-known lore. However, modern scholars believe that Sophocles invented a few of the play's characters himself. Southern Illinois University scholar Joan V. O'Brien suggests here that the playwright invented the central character, Antigone, himself, basing her personal story on tales told in his native village of Colonus (or Kolonos).

The interaction between the creative genius of the playwright and the mythic tradition is nowhere more fascinating and instructive than in this play. Some facts on the received myth about the sons of Oedipus and, more significantly, about the daughters of Oedipus shed light on Sophocles' relation to his material.

THE ROYAL BROTHERS

Our knowledge of the two brothers Polynices and Eteocles is meager and mostly dependent upon Aeschylus' *Seven against Thebes*, the third part of a trilogy on the ancestral curse on the house of Laios, produced about twenty-five years before the *Antigone*. Aeschylus' play focuses almost ex-

Excerpted from *Guide to Sophocles' "Antigone,"* by Joan V. O'Brien. Copyright © 1978 by Southern Illinois University Press. Reprinted by permission of Southern Illinois University Press.

clusively on Eteocles, initially the "rational," responsible, heroic leader of Thebes, who, like Creon, thinks of himself as the captain of the ship of state who must avoid female destruction, but who, unlike Creon, rises to tragic stature by his acceptance of his cursed fate as Oedipus' son. Subsequently, he goes out to meet Polynices in violent, unrestrained fratricidal [brother-killing] conflict. Nothing in the *Seven* elucidates the political or family background of the quarrel between the brothers. Neither Aeschylus nor Sophocles was interested in the reasons that Eteocles was the defender and Polynices the treasonous adversary. Nor does either play specify whether the two were twins, although the frequent use of duals may point in that direction. Only in Sophocles' much later *Oedipus at Kolonos* is a point made of their ages: there Polynices is made the elder son, presumably to strengthen his claim to the throne. Sophocles appears to have introduced this alteration of the myth into the *Oedipus at Kolonos* for the sake of the dramatic idea of that play.

Polynices never appears in the *Seven,* and on the rare occasions when he is mentioned it is as the villainous traitor. Eteocles, the more objective priest, and the Chorus see him thus. He is the one Eteocles must defeat, a man who lives up to his name (i.e., the "Much-Quarreler"), and yet a man whose shield claims that he like Eteocles has Justice on his side. The poet is not concerned to explore Polynices' claim since he focuses not on the conflict between the two but on the tragic heroism of Eteocles. When the Chorus calls Polynices an evil-spoken zealot, it is probably true that the phrase really characterizes both brothers.

Another tradition relating to the brothers was recorded in a lost Theban myth. This was the story of the *epigoni,* the sons of the Argive Seven, who unsuccessfully invaded Thebes. The sons succeeded where Polynices and their fathers failed.

Thus, as Sophocles received the myth, the brothers, perhaps twins, each claimed justice in his position, each appeared to be a mixture of good and evil, but Eteocles is considered Thebes' defender and Polynices the treasonous rebel.

THE ROYAL SISTERS

Sophocles' originality is far more significant in relation to the daughters of Oedipus. It is now generally agreed that he was the first to develop the story of the sisters and that he

was the creator of the character of his heroine. Homer, Hesiod, and Pindar do not mention the sisters at all in their ac-
counts of the myth, and the two scenes depicting them in the

AESCHYLUS'S VERSION OF ETEOCLES

In this excerpt from Aeschylus's Seven Against Thebes, *Eteocles, king of Thebes, addresses the citizens, warning them of an imminent attack on the city.*

ETEOCLES: Citizens, sons of Cadmus! The man who holds the helm
Of State, and from the bridge pilots with sleepless eyes
His country's fortunes, must speak what the hour demands.
If things go well, the thanks are due to Heaven; but if—
Which Heaven forbid!—ill-luck should meet us, Eteocles
Would be the one name harped upon in every street
With threats and wailings of indignant citizens;
From all which, may Zeus the Protector now protect
The city Cadmus founded! But you too must play
Your part. The youth still short of manhood, the old man
Whose prime is past—let both, nursing their vital force
To greatness, keep watch every way as duty calls;
Guard well your city, guard the altars of her gods,
That their due honour may not perish; guard your children,
And this dear earth, your mother and your nurse; for she,
When you were crawling infants, with her kindly soil
That bids all comers welcome, nourished you, and took
The burden of your upbringing, and made of you
Trustworthy men to found homes, carry shields, and grow
In strength and worth, able to answer this day's claim.

So far, the scale of fortune weighs upon our side,
Thanks to the gods, who through this lengthy time of siege
Have given to us the best of the war. But now our prophet,
Who keeps the augural birds and without help of fire
By hearing and reflection tells infallibly
The drift of portents—he, interpreting such signs,
Says that among the Achaeans a supreme attack
Is now this night being planned to overthrow our city.
Then, to the walls! Swarm to the battlements and gates;
Forward, full-armed; man parapets, fill every floor
Of every tower; and in the gate's mouth hold your ground
With courage. Never fear this horde of foreigners!

Philip Vellacott, trans., *Aeschylus:* Prometheus Bound, The Suppliants, Seven Against Thebes, The Persians. Baltimore: Penguin Books, 1961, pp. 88–89.

Seven against Thebes are now widely considered spurious later imitations inspired by Sophocles' play rather than sources for Sophocles as scholars used to think. Many of the key themes and even the vocabulary of Sophocles' drama appear in those scenes of Aeschylus: Antigone will find a way to bury her brother although she does not defend his act or character; . . . the strange power of the common womb from which they come . . . are curious echoes of the Sophoclean drama. But these themes, so integral to the *Antigone,* are handled as an afterthought in the *Seven.*

Therefore, may we not assume that the myth concerning Antigone's defiance of the king's order was probably a local legend in Sophocles' native Kolonos, just outside of Athens? Just as . . . Oedipus at Kolonos was probably part of the local tradition first developed in Sophocles' *Oedipus at Kolonos* (in the *Antigone,* Oedipus is thought of as dying in Thebes), so, too, local associations are probably the poet's source for the girl's act, the seed out of which his fertile imagination created the character of the heroine and the drama of her defiance. . . . Sophocles of Kolonos kept returning to the mysterious myth of his birthplace at widely separated moments in his career. He produced the *Antigone* in his fifties, the *Oedipus Tyrannos* over ten years later, and the *Oedipus at Kolonos* still twenty odd years after that. In all these works the mystery of birthplace and the mystery of creative genius interacted in a marvelous, one might say "deinotic" [strangely powerful or heroic] way.

The Play Has Two Central Characters

H.D.F. Kitto

In this essay, the noted and highly respected classical scholar H.D.F. Kitto points out that some of Sophocles' plays have one central character around whom most of the action of the story revolves. For instance, in *Oedipus Tyrannus* (*Oedipus the King*), Oedipus, king of Thebes, is the main character. Other plays by Sophocles, says Kitto, feature two central characters, an example being *Ajax*. *Antigone*, Kitto suggests, falls into the latter category, with Antigone and Creon sharing the main spotlight. However, it could be argued that one of these persons is somewhat more important than the other, and Kitto opts for Creon, calling it "the tragedy of Creon."

The *Antigone* is accused, though more gently, of the same fault as the *Ajax* [another of Sophocles' plays]: the heroine drops out half-way through and leaves us to do our best with Creon, Haemon, and their fortunes.

We must recognize that if there is a fault it is a radical one, due to deliberate choice and not to oversight or to the inability of Sophocles to cope with a difficult situation. It is inevitable that Antigone should disappear, but it is not inevitable that so little should be said in the Exodus about her, that her lover's corpse but not hers is brought back, that Creon should at such length lament his own fate, least of all that Eurydice should be so unexpectedly introduced in order to kill herself immediately. Why Eurydice? Sophocles had no Elizabethan relish for corpses. She is relevant only to Creon. Clearly the close of the play is all Creon, deliberately so, for there is less of Antigone than might have been. Sophocles is not even making the best of a bad job.

The difficulty that we feel arises from our regarding An-

Excerpted from *Greek Tragedy: A Literary Study*, by H.D.F. Kitto (Garden City, NY: Doubleday, 1952).

tigone as the chief character. If she is to this play what Oedipus and Electra are to theirs (and the *Antigone* is often criticized on this assumption), then the play is ill-balanced, but if the *Antigone* is more like the *Ajax* than the *Tyrannus,* the centre of gravity does not lie in one person, but between two. The *Ajax* is second-rate Sophocles until we feel the significance of Odysseus; the last part of the *Antigone* makes no sense until we realise that there is not one central character but two, and that of the two, the significant one to Sophocles was always Creon. It is simply a matter of looking at the dramatic facts. The older criticism (for of late things have taken a turn for the better) assumed that of course the play was about Antigone, and then set about explaining away the last scenes. The most satisfactory proof is performance. Creon can dominate the play.... But even without performance, we may note that Creon's part is half as long again as Antigone's, a point which is less mechanical than it sounds, and that it is the more dynamic part. Hers is impressive and affecting enough, but his has the wider range and is the more elaborate. Her fate is decided in the first few verses and she can but go to meet it; most of the dramatic forces used in the play are deployed against Creon—the slight reserve with which the chorus receives his edict, the news that he has been defied, and that too by a woman, the opposition of Haemon, the disapproval of the city, the supernatural machinery of Teiresias, the desertion of the chorus, the death of Haemon (foreshadowed), the death of Eurydice (unforeshadowed). Creon truly says

'Old sir, ye all like bowmen at a mark
Let fly your shafts at me.'

Antigone is indeed opposed, but not like this. Her tragedy is terrible, but it is foreseen and swift; Creon's grows before our eyes.

THE AUTHOR'S CHANGE OF OUTLOOK

This must have been the balance that Sophocles designed; whether this reading saves the play from fault is not our business. Perhaps modern minds make more of Antigone than was intended ... perhaps Antigone upset Sophocles' plans ... [but] it is most likely that Sophocles did precisely what he set out to do, and that in this play, as in the *Ajax,* he built on a double foundation.

As to this double foundation, in the change from the bipartite structure of the *Ajax*, through the much less prominent double interest of the *Antigone*, to the splendid unity of the *Tyrannus* and the *Electra*, it is natural for us to see a technical development; but something much more important than technique is involved, and it is not in fact easy to picture a Sophocles learning the rudiments of his art at the age of forty-five. Between these two earlier plays and the next two there is a perceptible change of tragic emphasis. The *Ajax* and the *Antigone* are based on what we may call a purely ethical conception; this way of life is right and that one is wrong: 'Not the thick-set and broad-shouldered prevail, but the wise, everywhere'; 'To be stiffnecked is folly.' Such a general idea naturally takes dramatic shape in an opposition between one who takes the wrong view and another who takes the right. In the second pair of plays the tragic idea is more philosophical, without of course ceasing to be ethical. One hero, more complex, more delicately poised, less catastrophic than either Ajax or Creon, fights not a moral law but his own nature. The moral and dramatic issue does not lie between him and another, but between the various facets of his own nature, assisted by the complexities of circumstance. Thus the one hero stands out more clearly from the other personages and a higher degree of unity follows. It is to some such fundamental change of outlook, not to the superficialities of dramatic technique, that we should turn if we wish to understand the development of Sophocles' form. Form, with him, is the same as thought....

CREON THE CHIEF AGENT

The *Antigone* has been variously interpreted. The transcendental philosophers, who, from Plato onwards, have never been at their ease with the tragic poets, have done their worst with it, and have been discomfited. It has been a problem-play, the poet's condemnation of contemporary statecraft, his confession of religious faith. What are the consequences of regarding it as primarily the tragedy of Creon?

First, I think we can afford to be reasonable about Antigone. [The early-nineteenth-century German philosopher Georg W.F.] Hegel had to assume that there was something seriously wrong with her; later critics, rejecting this preposterous view, were nevertheless careful to maintain (partly out of deference to Aristotle) that Antigone was not spotless. People are never spotless, especially heroes and heroines of tragedies. Antigone's hardness to Ismene therefore was exploited to the full—but this, surely, was no very striking blemish, hardly enough to spoil a perfect figure. . . . We need not be assiduous in looking for saving faults in Antigone, because only part of her character comes into question here, the part which impels her to defy Creon; and where the blemish is there, only Hegel can tell us. The play is not a full-length portrait of Antigone, in which, let it be granted, perfection would be a little uninteresting. Her part is to suffer, and there is no dramatic canon which demands that victims should have faults: hardness and decisiveness were given her to explain her rebellion and her suicide. The chief *agent* is Creon; his is the character, his the faults and merits, which are immediately relevant to the play. If Sophocles is really inviting us to watch Creon, Antigone becomes much more natural . . . no longer the standard-bearer of the Unwritten Laws. On this, the last day of her life, she can be spared faults, as she can be spared heroics.

HER BROTHER'S HONOR

Why indeed does she defy Creon? From a sense of religious duty? To Ismene, in the prologue, she mentions religious duty once—in an attempt to shame her sister. Her real thought comes out in phrases like

'He has no right to touch what is *mine!*—
Yes, my brother and—though you deny it—yours.'

She has a passionate feeling of what is due to her brother, to her race. Face to face with Creon's legality she indeed answers legally, and nobly, inspired to her highest eloquence, but essentially she is doing much more than championing one code against another; she is giving her whole being for her brother's honour. . . . The confrontation with Creon over, we hear little more of her religious faith; she protests her innocence indeed, but the burden of her defence is again that her brother is hers to honour. Her tone is noticeably more personal. As the end draws near her defences fail one by one, until, in that marvellously moving and tragic speech which was not to the taste of those who saw in Antigone chiefly a martyr to the Higher Law, she abandons everything except the fact that she did it and had to do it. Facing death, deserted by the Chorus, she has no confidence even in the gods, and doubts her own impulse. For a husband, she says, No; for a son, No; but for a brother. . . .

CREON'S FIELD OF ACTION

If Antigone is more interesting than a mere antithesis to Creon, he is more than the stubborn fool who kills her. Sophocles was interested in his fate. He is, if not cruel, at least insensitive; like a tyrant, he is quick to suspect, and he does not know how to yield. But he has his own honesty, his own justification, and his own sense of responsibility. But what Creon is is not the whole of the story. We have this clear-cut moral issue between him and Antigone—itself a little too elementary to serve as the sole background for so subtle a thinker as Sophocles. We have too the clear-cut personal clash; it is noteworthy that from the beginning of her confrontation Antigone shows her contempt for this court. She wastes no time in trying to bridge what she knows to be an impassable gap. But behind all this there is the evolving tragedy of Creon. Creon may be what you like, but he is neither unintelligent nor irresponsible. He has his own field of action and his own principles; impulse, unwritten laws, are, he feels, not for him; he cannot move in this ampler region, and he sincerely feels he has no business to. In his own field he has thought things out and is confident of himself. We feel his confidence as soon as we hear his

'Citizens, for what concerns the State . . .'

He has tradition and experience on his side, his maxims are sensible. True, a native stubbornness is given him, that he may defend his position to the dramatic end, but it is not from folly or wilfulness that he originally takes up his position. But his confident judgement was wrong; his reason betrays him. It is true that but for his obstinacy he could have escaped with a lighter penalty, but the bitterness is that his judgement was wrong, and that Antigone's instinct was right; and in the end he has less to cling to than she. She goes 'in the sure and certain hope That dear to thee will be my coming, Father'; he can say only

'Everything is turned to water in my hands.'

'By far the biggest part of happiness', says the Chorus, 'is Wisdom.' And what is this? Not to behave impiously towards the Gods is part of it. And what is this? Creon was honouring the Gods after his fashion, Antigone after hers. How can you tell beforehand which is the right fashion? Alas! Piety is not an automatic thing. . . . This is the tragedy of Creon.

Ismene Is Motivated by Love for Her Sister

G.M. Kirkwood

Former Cornell University scholar G.M. Kirkwood, a noted authority on ancient Greek literature, here examines Ismene's character by comparing her motives and ideals to Antigone's. Ultimately, he explains, Ismene, like her more audacious sister, shows courage, which is inspired by her deep love for Antigone.

Antigone and Ismene are together in two scenes, in the prologue and at the end of the second episode. The contrast between them is not that of devotion to a cause *vs.* timidity; it is more complex than that and more revealing of the character of Antigone. Of course Antigone is devoted and has a cause; and Ismene, by contrast, is timid. But to what, exactly, is Antigone's devotion, and what does it indicate about her? The contrast with Ismene helps us to answer these questions.

DEVOTION TO A NOBLE NATURE

In the prologue Antigone's first concern is not for religious duty, which looms so large in her scene with Creon. Her first reaction is a personal one; the matter is one of family loyalty, where, she feels, Creon has no right to intrude. Antigone is intense, as we see from the opening line on; her greeting to Ismene has more of intimacy and passion than of loving gentleness. To Creon's clumsy interference with her duty to her family, she responds with instinctive hostility. She is furious that Creon should seek to legislate to her in a matter so personal to her: "Such conditions they say the worthy Creon has proclaimed for you and me—yes, even for me"! The burial of Polyneices becomes for her the very touchstone of nobility, and she declares that Ismene by her attitude toward it will show "Whether you are of noble na-

Excerpted from *A Study of Sophoclean Drama*, by G.M. Kirkwood. Copyright ©1958 by Cornell University Press. Used by permission of Cornell University Press.

ture or base though your parents were good"....Antigone has an unhesitating devotion to her concept of what is becoming to [that noble nature]. . . .

ISMENE'S PRUDENCE

Up to this point Antigone has not reflected and has not formulated her instinctive idealism. She is not to be thought of as primarily a philosopher or an embodiment of the reasoned way of life. By the contrasting reaction of Ismene we understand more clearly what Antigone is. Ismene's conduct is equally instinctive. Suddenly confronted with a bold and illegal scheme, she shrinks at once, for her instinct is to obey, just as surely as Antigone's is to exercise her own will: she is a woman, and cannot fight against men; she must obey; Antigone's plan lacks common sense; those below will forgive her for not acting. . . . So far as moral attitude is concerned, there is no fundamental difference; Ismene is as aware as Antigone of the wrongness of Creon's edict. The difference is in personality: Ismene is without the imperiousness, willfulness, and single-mindedness of her sister; she is prudent and sees other aspects of the situation. Antigone has eyes for only the one issue that is to her all-important.

THE INSPIRATION FOR ISMENE'S COURAGE

There is another contrast between them. When Ismene shows reluctance to act, Antigone becomes instantly hostile. She declares bitterly that she would not now accept her sister's help if it were offered; when Ismene advises silence and says that she too will be silent about the plan to bury Polyneices, Antigone angrily bids her tell it to all. Antigone promises Ismene the hatred of their dead brother and of herself; Ismene in the last words of the prologue assures Antigone of her love, mad though she may be. It is Ismene, then, who has . . . the gentleness and affection and patience. . . . Relatively, Antigone is hard, abrupt, intolerant, and in this she is like Ajax [the stubborn title character of an earlier play by Sophocles]. It is the natural concomitant and price of her firmness and singlemindedness.

The second incident continues the contrast. To Ismene's unexpected and courageous attempt to assume joint responsibility for the burial and to share the punishment, Antigone's response is a passionate rejection. Both reactions are, super-

ISMENE OFFERS TO DIE WITH ANTIGONE
This translation of the crucial scene between Ismene and Antigone is by the noted scholar Robert Fagles.

CREON:

You—

in my own house, you viper, slinking undetected,
sucking my life-blood! I never knew
I was breeding twin disasters, the two of you
rising up against my throne. Come, tell me,
will you confess your part in the crime or not?
Answer me. Swear to me.

ISMENE:

I did it, yes—

if only she consents—I share the guilt,
the consequences too.

ANTIGONE:

No,

Justice will never suffer that—not you,
you were unwilling. I never brought you in.

ISMENE:

But now you face such dangers . . . I'm not ashamed
to sail through trouble with you,
make your troubles mine.

ANTIGONE:

Who did the work?

Let the dead and the god of death bear witness!
I have no love for a friend who loves in words alone.

ISMENE:

Oh no, my sister, don't reject me, please,
let me die beside you, consecrating
the dead together.

ANTIGONE:

Never share my dying,

don't lay claim to what you never touched.
My death will be enough.

ISMENE:

What do I care for life, cut off from you?

Robert Fagles, trans., *Sophocles: The Three Theban Plays:* Antigone, Oedipus the King, Oedipus at Colonus. New York: Penguin Books, 1984, pp. 86–87.

ficially, strange; but both are in place. We soon learn Ismene's reason: so warmly does she love her sister that she
cannot face life without her, and this is what inspires her
with courage. Antigone's conduct is a continuation of what
we saw in the prologue. The harshness with which she here
spurns Ismene is no different from her impetuous scorn
there. Antigone knows that Ismene is even yet not in real
sympathy with her spirit. For Ismene is acting out of affection; Antigone's drive comes instead from her concept, at first
intuitive, now formulated, of noble conduct.

ANTIGONE CASTS ASIDE NORMALITY

Does Antigone suffer by the contrast? As a specimen of normal, gentle womanhood, perhaps she does. But it is a part of
her towering strength to cast aside such normality.... Critics who want an Antigone against whom no breath of criticism can be uttered tend to undervalue the interplay between the protagonist and her sister; [one noted critic] saw
in their second meeting only an effort by Antigone to save Ismene from death, disregarding the whole atmosphere and
nearly all the implications of the incident. But we shall not
understand Sophocles' protagonists by closing our eyes to
those aspects of their portrayal that do not satisfy our pre-
conceived specifications.

The Role of the Gods

Cedric H. Whitman

Although the Greek gods do not make a physical appearance in *Antigone*, their presence, or at least their
moral indignation and guidance, is felt through the
character of the seer Teiresias. He warns Creon that
the divine Olympians will not look kindly on his order to leave the dead Polynices unburied. The following discussion of the indirect role the gods play in
the story is by a noted authority on Sophocles and
his works, Cedric H. Whitman, former instructor of
Greek and Latin at Harvard University.

The falling action of the tragedy is not without its puzzle, for
with the entrance of Teiresias, presumably, a whole new set
of agents appear. These are, of course, the gods, whose pres-
ences are felt in the person of the seer. He has little character
outside of the specific message he brings: that Creon must
reverse his decree and save Antigone, for the gods are angry.
At face value, this seems a little melodramatic, an eleventh-
hour arrival of rescue. The common assumption is that the
gods here assert themselves in the interest of justice. Yet if
one interprets the Teiresias scene thus, the conclusion
inevitably follows that the gods, who are supposed to be justifying their existence, are either malign or hopelessly in-
competent. By the time they move, the holocaust of self-
destruction has already taken place. If this is indeed the gods'
action, their sudden appearance is a little like the proverbial
coward who boasts about a battle for which he came too late.
On the other hand, if they merely wished to punish Creon,
there was no need to send Teiresias, or do anything at all, for
the steps in the human action are all perfectly self-sufficient:
Creon kills Antigone, Haemon in despair kills himself, and
Eurydice, who enters solely to add her drop of gall to Creon's
cup, takes her own life in sorrow for her son. One may or
may not take this as a lesson from the gods and a sign of their

justice; the chorus certainly does. But if it is the gods' doings, then the gods have hidden themselves in tragic masks and acted wholly through the actors. Why does Teiresias come, and why are the gods involved at all? Taken literally, neither their justice nor their omnipotence appears from the closing scenes, but rather the opposite.

GIVING THE ACTION A COSMIC SETTING

The answer seems to lie . . . in Sophocles' use of the gods—that is, the Olympian deities—as symbols. By letting them speak only after the action is complete, he carefully divorces them from any suspicion of causation or interference. But they still, of their very augustness, bear witness, for the world at large, to the truth and significance of the heroic action. Thus no responsibility is removed from the actors, and their psychology is not violated but magnified by reference to figures out of eternity. Such divine or semidivine persons, who are themselves outside the action, picture it for us whole. They show no more than the action has shown, but they give it a cosmic setting. For Teiresias, the blind seer, the sputtering of the altar flames and the shrieking of the birds are signs of heavenly displeasure, of a time out of joint. He senses an unholy crime and hastens to tell his fear. In so many words, he states that it is a sacrilege to invert nature, to leave the dead Polyneices unburied, and bury Antigone alive. But it is for Creon to act. Teiresias confirms Antigone's rightness; but he could not have done so without her death. It was her standard, her moral belief from the first, which has now become the concern of life in the larger sense; if it was divine in her, it now returns more universally divine, under the guise of "the gods." But nothing new has happened, except that Creon is now able to look in a mirror large enough and authoritative enough so that even he cannot mistake the fatal outline of his own deed and the justice of Antigone's. Had Teiresias come sooner, or had Creon's change of heart been sufficient to rescue the innocent, we might say that the gods came down from heaven and interfered. But they meant no such thing. They intended neither justice nor a display of power when they refused the sacrifice; they meant only to show how things were.

THEIR INSCRUTABLE SECRET

Choice, action, suffering, and death are the domain of humanity. The gods do not enter it—at least, not in Sophocles.

All motive comes from within the actors, and only in the sense of an inward moral standard, which is itself a kind of divinity, can any god be called responsible for Antigone's death. It is she who drives the action and wills her death. Similarly, Creon's actions rise exclusively from character, the character of a tyrant, and in the end he suffers not for a standard, but for a loss. He devises his own punishment, as Antigone devises her own glory.

One must be wary with Sophocles. The express approval or disapproval of the gods, introduced directly into the action, may seem to mean more than it does. We did not need the gods to tell us Antigone was right, though doubtless Creon did. Moreover, the approval of the gods upon her deed lends no hint in this play as to who the gods really are, or what sort of divinity has set its seal upon her moral position. In the last analysis, the gods whom Teiresias represents, though presumably in some sense the governors of the universe, remain in the midst of their inscrutable [impenetrable] secret, and serve only to illuminate once more the greatness of Antigone. . . . They are mere symbolic coefficients of the human sphere. . . . But it is impossible to determine as yet the nature of the larger divine world which swings partly into view in the final scene, nor is the relation of this larger world to the godlike dynamic inner force even dimly broached. But already in the *Antigone* it is possible to observe the kind of heroic action through which the poet hinted at this relation for many years before he was able to define it more fully in *Oedipus at Colonus.*

CHAPTER 4

Modern Adaptations of *Antigone* Reevaluate Its Themes and Characters

READINGS ON
ANTIGONE

A Modern Antigone Strives for an Unattainable Purity

John Harvey

A number of modern playwrights have composed their own versions of Antigone's story, based on Sophocles' original. As might be expected, these plays invariably use the ancient Greek model as a backdrop on which they superimpose contemporary emotional, moral, political, and cultural situations and dilemmas. Perhaps the most famous modern version of *Antigone* is by the French dramatist Jean Anouilh (1910–1987), written in 1944 and set in World War II France. Anouilh used the same characters and situations as Sophocles did. But the modern versions of the characters undergo somewhat different emotional developments. As literary scholar and Anouilh authority John Harvey explains in this essay, for example, Anouilh injects a more modern spirit into the play's climax. The playwright takes his Antigone beyond the Sophoclean dilemma of family-versus-community obligations to what is for her a startling realization about her destiny.

Perhaps it is in *Antigone* that Anouilh has most successfully met the dramaturgical problems raised by his concept of tragedy. Here ... the action is irrevocably enclosed in a theatrical frame: a prologue-character introduces the spectators to the members of the cast about to replay their tragedy. There is nothing anyone can do, he says in formulas which by now have become household words; they must all play their parts to the end.

A FEELING OF FATALITY

Once the prologue has settled the matter of predestination, the lights are lowered, the stage cleared, and the story al-

Excerpted from *Anouilh: A Study in Theatrics*, by John Harvey (New Haven, CT: Yale University Press). Copyright ©1964 by Yale University. Reprinted with permission of the publisher.

lowed to unfold realistically. And yet a feeling of fatality pervades the entire performance. It is maintained both by means of intermittent self-conscious lines (e.g. "Each has his role. He has to put us to death, and we have to bury our brother. That's the way the parts were given") and by means of a forceful intrusion of the chorus later in the play. Whereas the chorus and the audience may understand the fatality, the characters do not: Hémon has no idea what is happening, Créon is convinced he can save Antigone, and the heroine herself is (at first) interested only in burying her brother. But as the play builds to a climax—and here Anouilh's genius reaches full sway—heroine and spectator alike uncover the true meaning of her role. Her destiny is not, as everyone has believed all along, to subordinate civil obligations to those of family or religion. Créon lets slip a few words in praise of everyday happiness and all is over: Antigone pounces on these words, and in a flurry of rhetoric she suddenly understands that her role is to reject compromise, to spurn all life which is less than perfection.

ARGUMENT LEADS TO SELF-REVELATION

What more may be said about Antigone's illumination? To begin with, it is a highly dramatic turnabout, because it comes on the heels of her virtual acquiescence to Créon. Secondly, it is plausible, because it has arisen not from a lovers' quarrel . . . but from an altercation pitting earthly order against divine duty. And finally, it is psychologically convincing, because it follows an intense and exhausting argument, in which . . . the very heat of argument has led to self-revelation. This was intentional: Anouilh had his chorus introduce the key scene between Antigone and Créon with these words: "there is nothing left but to shout—not moan, no, nor complain—but to howl, at the top of your lungs, the things you've always wanted to say and never have and which perhaps you never even knew before now. And for nothing: just to say them to yourself, just to learn them, yourself."

CRÉON'S AWAKENING

Concerning Créon's role, it may be noted that, while the first audiences in 1944 reviled him as a collaborationist, many have since come to regard him, and not Antigone, as the true hero of this tragedy of character. The prologue informs us that Créon has already felt ashamed of his base "official" acts, that he has adopted as a . . . blind and mechanical performance of duty. Hence, throughout the climactic scene both he and Antigone admit that, somehow, it is he who is in the wrong. Toward the end of their grueling encounter,

---

THE CHORUS PREDICTS THE TRAGEDY TO COME

This is the opening speech of Anouilh's Antigone, *in which the chorus introduces the characters (who can be seen on-stage) and foreshadows their downfalls.*

ANTIGONE, *her hands clasped round her knees, sits on the top step. The* THREE GUARDS *sit on the steps, in a small group, playing cards. The* CHORUS *stands on the top step.* EURYDICE *sits on the top step, just left of center, knitting. The* NURSE *sits on the second step, left of* EURYDICE. ISMENE *stands in front of arch, left, facing* HAEMON, *who stands left of her.* CREON *sits in the chair at right end of the table, his arm over the shoulder of his* PAGE, *who sits on the stool beside his chair. The* MESSENGER *is leaning against the downstage portal of the right arch.*

The curtain rises slowly; then the CHORUS *turns and moves downstage.*

CHORUS. Well, here we are.

These people are about to act out for you the story of Antigone.

That thin little creature sitting by herself, staring straight ahead, seeing nothing, is Antigone. She is thinking. She is thinking that the instant I finish telling you who's who and what's what in this play, she will burst forth as the tense, sallow, willful girl whose family would never take her seriously and who is about to rise up alone against Creon, her uncle, the King.

Another thing that she is thinking is this: she is going to die. Antigone is young. She would much rather live than die. But there is no help for it. When your name is Antigone, there is only one part you can play; and she will have to play hers through to the end.

From the moment the curtain went up, she began to feel that inhuman forces were whirling her out of this world, snatching her away from her sister Ismene, whom you see smiling and chatting with that young man; from all of us who sit or stand here, looking at her, not in the least upset ourselves—for we are not doomed to die tonight.

Jean Anouilh, *Works.* 3 vols. New York: Hill and Wang, 1958, vol. 1, p. 3.

Créon seems to awaken to the value of life itself, no matter how imperfect. But it is not until his shattering clash with Hémon that, pushed to the limit, forced to defend his actions before the accusing eyes of his son, Créon finally realizes that accepting life does not mean complacency in the face of all its horrors as one clutches at meager happiness; he realizes that to accept life is to accept being a man, to shed the comforts of infantile dreams, and to behold for once the world in all its beauty *and* ugliness.

EMBRACING THE UNACCEPTABLE

Antigone is the tragedy of a girl who aspires to a purity beyond life itself. Life is unacceptable for her, and purity unattainable. The heroine, precast into a part which demanded death, is able to transfigure her role to tragic proportions by dying for this purity. The hero—for thus we may call Créon—equally aspires to the ideal, but finds himself thrust into the role of king, weighed down not only by his own life but by the lives of his subjects as well. He, too, plays his part tragically, by embracing the unacceptable.

Brecht's *Antigone* Emphasizes Contemporary Rather than Universal Ideals

Keith A. Dickson

Bertolt Brecht (1898–1956) was an innovative German poet and playwright whose works had a major influence on twentieth-century drama and theater production. Like many other modern writers, critics, and intellectuals, he was drawn to Sophocles' *Antigone* because of the timeless qualities of its story, themes, and characters. And like other playwrights, including France's celebrated Jean Anouilh, Brecht crafted his own version of the ancient play. (Brecht's version was first produced in 1947, three years after Anouilh's.) Brecht emphasized the political confrontation between Antigone and Creon, giving it a contemporary spin reflecting the grim realities of the control of his native Germany by the Nazis in the 1930s and 1940s. Creon is portrayed as a completely unsympathetic tyrant, much like Nazi dictator Adolf Hitler, and Antigone as a political demonstrator. In this essay, excerpted from his insightful study of Brecht's works, University of Exeter scholar Keith A. Dickson maintains that Brecht's version of the play ultimately fails because it deals more with topical politics than with universal human experience.

The *Antigone* of Sophocles was a natural target for Brecht's practical criticism of the classics. . . . It is, moreover, one of the most politically orientated plays in the classical repertoire, and for good measure it was the favourite play of Brecht's favourite philosopher, [the early-nineteenth-century German philosopher Georg W.F.] Hegel.

From *Toward Utopia: A Study of Brecht*, by Keith A. Dickson (Oxford: Clarendon Press). Copyright © Keith A. Dickson 1978. Reprinted by permission of Oxford University Press.

What makes *Antigone* just as exciting and just as relevant today as when it was first produced in Athens in 441 B.C. is the head-on collision of two irreconcilable absolutes: the flagrant humanity of Antigone, who sees intuitively what is eternally right, and Creon's argument from political expediency, backed by the coercive power of the state.

Hegel saw in this conflict the dialectical process of history. For him the absolute *Weltgeist* [civilized human mind, or spirit], incarnate in Creon as ruler and in Antigone as individual conscience, is divided against itself, and thus what Sophocles had unconsciously dramatized was not the conflict of good with evil, but of one kind of good with another. . . . Creon was right in Hegel's view to maintain the integrity of the state at all costs, but Antigone was equally right to oppose it in the interests of individuation. Both of them are the tragic victims of historical necessity.

NATURE'S LAW FLOUTED

Hegel overrated the sympathy that Sophocles elicits for his clumsy despot. [Noted classical scholar] Maurice Bowra has argued persuasively that the rhythm of the play ensures a gradual swing of sympathy away from Creon towards Antigone. The subordinate status of women in ancient society, concern for the stability of the city-state, and a deeply rooted respect for authority must have made Creon's condemnation of Antigone's headstrong individualism seem very plausible to a Greek audience. On the other hand, an equally deep-rooted reverence for the dead—the Athenians buried even their inveterate enemies at Marathon—and unquestioning recognition of the unwritten laws which Antigone invokes in defence of her actions must also have fostered a growing suspicion that she is right after all. Creon's inflexibility is not, however, the product of wilful despotism. It is the result of inexperience and insecurity. As he ironically says himself in his opening speech it is only in office that a man shows his true mettle, and he has been in office less than a day when he is required to make his first and last political decision: how to control the warring factions that have just rent Thebes. In refusing burial to Polynices he makes the wrong decision and he is too unsure of himself to risk revoking it. Creon forfeits more and more of our sympathy as he allows personal acrimony to cloud his judgement . . . in condemning Antigone to a barbarous death. By punishing her instinctive piety so cruelly and by misinterpreting his son's response to it as wanton defiance of his authority, Creon has flouted an immutable law of nature which exacts a terrible vengeance. This law, stronger than any of Creon's decrees, impels Antigone, Haemon, and Eurydice to their untimely deaths, and Creon is left to live with his guilt. As Creon's world shatters about him and his pride breaks, the pendulum of sympathy swings back the other way. Antigone and Creon are both tragic figures in their own right, but it is Creon who dominates the stage despite the title of the play. Antigone's tragedy is the measure of his own. The Chorus pronounce Sophocles' own gloomy verdict in their final summing-up:

> Wisdom is the first prerequisite
> Of happiness. No man may neglect
> Due reverence towards the gods. Great blows
> Requite the great speeches of the proud
> And in old age teach wisdom.

Man is educable, it seems, but all too often the experience by which he learns crushes him.

THE SETTING OF BRECHT'S MODERN VERSION

Such was the temper of Sophocles' finest work. Brecht's adaptation of it, like Anouilh's, was consciously a product of the Second World War. Although it was written (in less than a fortnight) for a provincial Swiss theatre in Chur at the end of 1947, it looks back to the recent war mainly for the benefit of a German public.

Brecht made it abundantly clear that he had turned to the ancient myth not in order to recreate the spirit of antiquity, but 'because its subject-matter facilitated a certain degree of topicality'. If the Chur production retained many features of antique theatrical practice—a chorus, masks, more or less authentic costumes, even a sense of amphitheatrical breadth and depth in the staging—Brecht was aiming largely at alienation, not authenticity. To the bewilderment of the Swiss audience, who had seen nothing of Brecht's Epic Theatre in their provincial backwater, he . . . [also used] a gong, a gramophone with music recorded from a specially doctored piano, a table for incidental props, a bench for the actors to sit on between entrances, and all this in full view of the audience. A brightly lit curtainless stage which exposed the scene-shifting, together with the then unfamiliar 'epic' style of acting, which involved addressing many of the lines

directly to the audience, completes the tally of devices introduced 'to prevent the audience from feeling transported to
the scene of the action'. The beauty of ancient myth was not
to be allowed to induce oblivion of the recent past, 'Memo-
ries of the late war beguiling / Into slumber sound', as the
Sophoclean Chorus sing. . . .

"Kreon's War"

The Chur production had begun with what Brecht described
as an 'Aktualitätspunkt', namely a rather banal prologue in
rhymed doggerel, acted out on a skeletal set in front of the
already visible classical stage. A placard lowered from the
flies announced that the date is March 1945 and the place
Berlin. Two sisters await the now inevitable defeat of Germany as the Russians close in on Berlin. A brother has deserted the army and is hanged by the S.S. Thinking he may
still be alive, one of the sisters goes to cut him down, risking
arrest for complicity. At the sound of a gong the two ac-
tresses, Helene Weigel and Marita Glenck, handed their
coats to an assistant and returned as Antigone and Ismene
respectively to play their opening scene.

Although Brecht's *Antigone* is not primarily an anti-war
play, the war-theme was amplified into a major issue in order to accentuate the topical relevance. In Sophocles' version it merely serves to motivate Creon's act of terrorism.
Polynices, raising an army in Argos against his brother Eteocles, has attacked his native Thebes, and the hostile brothers
have killed each other in battle the night before the action
begins. Creon feels justified in taking drastic measures to
suppress anarchy, anticipating opposition to his succession
as next of kin. He finds himself in the invidious position of
having to victimize a kinsman to deter other would-be
rebels, and his discomfiture is further increased when another member of his ill-fated family is the first to call his
bluff. Memory of the recent war forces Creon to abide by his
rash decision, but from this point on the war-theme has out-
lived its usefulness and is dropped.

In Brecht's adaptation war is the ground bass of the entire
action, and the Chur production emphasized this by replacing the traditional fluted pillars with four totem-poles bearing the skulls of horses, which marked off the acting area of
the stage. Kreon's campaign against Argos, which has obvious parallels with Germany's invasion of Russia, is no longer

a defensive war, but an act of aggression against a powerful rival. But even the economic motive is little more than a pretext for Kreon. He needs Argive ore to boost his sagging economy, but he also needs the war as such to distract the attention of his subjects from the gross mismanagement responsible for the crisis. Just as historians often refer to the Second World War as Hitler's war, so Antigone, Hämon, and eventually even the Theban elders speak of this war as Kreon's. At one point, seeking to justify repressive measures really designed to shore up a corrupt regime, Kreon asks Antigone, 'Is there no war?', and Antigone replies simply, 'Yes, yours'.

ANTIGONE A POLITICAL DEMONSTRATOR?

This shift in emphasis, seemingly unimportant in itself, has a disastrous effect on the characterization and ultimately also on the scale of values by which the basic issues of the play are judged. In the traditional version Polynices is a traitor to a cause with which the audience is encouraged to identify itself. No audience questions Creon's right to captain the ship of state of which he speaks in his famous opening speech. It merely learns to criticize his faulty navigation. In this light Creon's notorious edict does not at first appear unduly repressive. On the contrary, it is Antigone's defiance of it that is intended to seem wilful. In Brecht's version, however, Polyneikes was not killed by his war-hero of a brother but by the fanatical Kreon himself, ostensibly for cowardly desertion, but in fact for having realized the insanity of a war in which his own brother has just died so pointlessly. Whereas Sophocles' audience is Theban in its loyalties, Brecht's is against Kreon's Thebes from the start. This makes the outraged Polyneikes a hero of the resistance, and Antigone's symbolic burial of him is no longer an act of stubborn personal loyalty to a traitor, but a political demonstration. As a member of the ruling classes, Antigone has been brought by the course of the war to realize that this power-crazed tyrant has set the ship of state, in which both she and the Elders have a vested interest, on a course that is bound to end in disaster. . . .

The rightness of Antigone's stand against tyranny no longer needs divine endorsement from the mouth of Teiresias, the blind seer. It is borne out by the military defeat of Kreon's creaking war-machine. Instead of the Messenger's moving account of the deaths of Antigone, Haemon, and Eurydice, we have a dying war-correspondent's eyewitness report on the enemy's heroic defence of Argos—at this point a transparent cipher for Stalingrad—in the face of which Kreon's army, led by his other son Megareus (whom Sophocles only mentioned in passing), has lost heart and suffered a crushing defeat. Kreon now faces the inevitable counterattack, his striking-power on the home front paralysed by the desertion of Hämon. The play ends with the doomed Kreon anticipating an orgy of destruction.

CREON'S TRAGIC DIMENSION ELIMINATED

[Literary critic] Ronald Gray has aptly described Brecht's Kreon as 'a flatly rapacious caricature of Hitler'. The character defects of Sophocles' tyrant are many and obvious, but they are the weaknesses of mediocrity, not the vices of a criminal superman. A sympathetic bungler becomes in Brecht's version a seasoned bully and a frenzied monomaniac, 'the public figure and bloody clown', as Brecht himself put it. Even with his political ambitions in ruins he is not an object of tragic pity. In Brecht's notes on the play the question: 'Is Kreon to win the sympathy of the audience in his misfortune?' receives the monosyllabic answer, 'No.'

Brecht's treatment of Hämon was dictated by the same principle. The Sophoclean youth is headstrong and impulsive, passionately in love with Antigone and gradually roused to open defiance of his father. The Chorus notes that his actions are controlled by Aphrodite [goddess of love], and this should have given pause to Creon. But by now Creon is blinded by anger and is only brought to his senses by the intervention of Teiresias. When he arrives at the tomb too late to save Antigone, his son spits in his face and attacks him with his sword before killing himself in despair. This terrible experience and the subsequent death of his wife, Eurydice, bring Creon tragic insight. There are few scenes in ancient drama more moving than our final glimpse of the broken and contrite Creon as he mourns his dead son:

> Lead me away, a worthless wretch,
> Who unwittingly slew you, my son,
> And her too. Unhappy that I am, I know not
> Which way to turn. All paths lead astray.
> Upon my head a crushing fate has fallen.

By contrast, Brecht's Kreon mourns the death of Hämon only

because it follows hard upon the death of Megareus, leaving him with no hope of organizing a final stand against the advancing Argives. The thwarted architect of a millennial empire, like Hitler, he braces himself for the end. . . . Add to this the fact that Eurydice has been omitted from the cast-list altogether, and it will be seen that Brecht has eliminated the human dimension of Creon's tragic error, which dominates the action of Sophocles' play.

This is the most serious fault of Brecht's adaptation. Though he furnished no evidence in support of his claim, Brecht maintained that he had reconstructed the pre-Sophoclean folk-legend and that, in the foreseeable future, audiences which have learned to read both history and literature dialectically [logically] would be able to see in Sophocles' original play all that his adaptation had made of it. Despite this ambitious claim it is safe to predict that the sophisticated audiences of Utopia are more likely to condemn Brecht's rationalized *Antigone* as an evisceration [gutting] of Sophocles' myth.

SUPERNATURAL ELEMENTS

Sophocles' *Antigone* is a profoundly religious play. This is not to say that it concedes to the gods any prescriptive right to intervene in human affairs, for the supernatural as such has no part in it. It is just that in moments of crisis the noblest of men apprehend another dimension of their mutual relationship, inexplicable in terms of reason and expediency. No rational argument can explain away human reverence for the dead, and Antigone's deepest instincts tell her to give her brother the burial that Creon has denied him. She is not a martyr to an abstract rational principle. One commentator has said: 'Antigone has no reason; she has only her instinct', and another, writing at the same time as Brecht: 'her resolve sprang from an impulse of pure love, not from a calculation or a sense of duty to the family or even a religious scruple'. Antigone herself says simply to Creon: 'I was born for fellowship in love, not fellowship in hate'. A deep awareness of human kinship and human dignity motivate Antigone's defiance of Creon, and it is in this sense that her motives can be described as religious. [Renowned scholar] H.D.F. Kitto has written of them: 'The religious and the human or instinctive motives are not sharply distinguished by Sophocles, indeed they are fused—and for a very good reason: he saw no distinction between them; the fundamental laws of humanity and . . . of the gods are the same thing'.

If there is a sense of the numinous [supernatural] about Sophocles' *Antigone* it is not because Teiresias, whom Brecht reduces to a crafty amateur politician, is the spokesman of the gods. Teiresias merely confirms what Antigone and Haemon already know and what Creon and the Elders find out through bitter experience: Nature itself has laws with which Creon's conflict. Creon's basic failure, the commonest fault of all doctrinaire politicians, is . . . technically irreverence towards the gods, but in the final analysis a fatal disregard for the ultimate claims of humanity. A line from Sophocles' other great study in tyranny aptly describes the laws which govern Antigone's actions: 'There is a great god in them, who grows not old'.

WHY BRECHT'S VERSION FAILS

The universality of Sophocles' drama rests on just this sense of the numinous. Despite the studied topicality of his adaptation, Brecht also strove for universality, and he too would have claimed that he had exposed the underlying laws of nature, only he sought them not in human response but in economic causality. He realized himself that his *Antigone* comes perilously close to a kind of morality play, illustrating the banal maxim 'Crime does not pay.' Unlike the original, it is basically optimistic, showing, he believed, 'that political enterprises demanding excessive violence are likely to founder'. Kreon's lust for power has, like Hitler's, overtaxed the resources of the state and so precipitated its internal decay. There are no 'unwritten laws' in Brecht's version, which discreetly omits the passage in which Antigone refers to them. The politically farsighted Antigone, Teiresias, and Hämon demonstrate against what amounts to a strategic blunder in the class war rather than an outrage against humanity. . . .

Brecht was quite wrong to suppose that Sophocles' play was apolitical. Indeed it was political in the original sense, for it was an essay on the nature of the πόλις [polis, i.e., the city-state or community] and the dangers that beset it:

Creon   Am I to rule this land by any other will than mine?

Haemon A city that belongs to one man only is no city at all. . . .

Kitto has written of Sophocles: 'His political experiences and judgments passed through his mind and when they came out, they were transmuted into something else—into that highest form of art which has contemplated and then can illuminate, human experience.' This is precisely where Brecht's adaptation so signally fails, despite its ingenuity. Brecht's *Antigone* is not about human experience at all, but about political abstractions, from which no society, least of all Utopia, can be constructed.

Two Contemporary Antigones Retain the Noble Qualities of Sophocles' Heroine

Anna Krajewska-Wieczorek

The following essay is an analysis by literary scholar and critic Anna Krajewska-Wieczorek of two of the most recent modern versions of Sophocles' *Antigone.* The first is Griselda Gambaro's *Antigona Furiosa,* first produced in Buenos Aires, Argentina, in 1986, the other Janusz Glowacki's *Antigone in New York,* which had its premiere in Washington, D.C., in 1993. According to Krajewska-Wieczorek, Gambaro's play compares Antigone's grief for her dead brother to that of Argentina's mothers for the loss of loved ones who disappeared under that nation's oppressive government in the 1980s. Glowacki's version, by contrast, is set in the slums of modern New York City. Its heroine, though low-class and poor, displays the same dedication to the memory of a loved one as did the original Antigone. In both of these newer versions, the heroines possess the same independent spirit as their ancient counterpart, proving once more that what made Sophocles great was his ability to create characters and situations that transcend time and place.

From the time of Sophocles' *Antigone,* his version of the myth—which relates how Oedipus' daughter buried her brother Polyneices against the decree of Creon and, upon being sentenced to death, died by her own hand—became invariable. It was in modern treatments of the story that changes began to be introduced: these concerned the person or authorities representing the law; the time when the events occur, and their location; the person whom Antigone

Reprinted from Anna Krajewska-Wieczorek, "Two Contemporary Antigones," *New Theater Quarterly,* vol. 10, no. 40 (November 1994), pp. 327–30, by permission of the author.

buries; and why she dies. But a continuing, necessary determinant in such modern incarnations of the myth has been the conflict between the ethos of authority and the ethos of moral belief—this latter being motivated by religion, duty to the family, or love. Without such an opposition, *Antigone* loses its ground as tragedy.

The motif of madness in the classical version of *Antigone* has been widely discussed. In three instances in the play Sophocles' heroine is reproved for acting unreasonably, and warned of punishment within the authoritarian system. Antigone's decisions and actions were, then, judged to be irrational and perceived as acts of madness from the point of view of the establishment. The opposition between madness and normal behaviour had its roots in the jurisdiction of that controlled society: but Antigone is not condemned for madness in the ethical realm which transcends the disciplines of institutionalized authority.

OF SHATTERED MIND

The idea that ethics can be a dominating motive of existence regardless of the political structure or rules governing a society becomes central in two recent plays based on the myth of Antigone: Griselda Gambaro's *Antigona Furiosa* and Janusz Glowacki's *Antigone in New York*—in both of which Antigone is out of her wits: 'insane', 'mad', 'crazy'.

These two modern Antigones—one brought to life again in Argentina, the other in New York—are openly divorced from reality, oblivious of the law. In the first case this is represented by Argentinian society in the 1980s, oppressed by a military government; in the second, the homeless and 'outlaws' of the 1990s are maintaining a 'delicate balance between civil rights and civil order' in New York's Thompkins Square. Although thus distanced in time, both contemporary Antigones remain faithful to the essential feature of the Sophoclean archetype in their mission of love.

The most striking trait of both contemporary Antigones is their 'fazed' personality, an internal drive which is manifested in external symptoms of insanity. It is the theatrical effect of Ophelia as she appears in Act IV of *Hamlet* with her bouquet of flowers—as Laertes puts it, 'a document in madness, thoughts and remembrance fitted'.

Gambaro's short play opens with her Antigona locked in a gigantic cage, hanged. On stage she must look like a dead bird forgotten by her owners, or starved. 'In her hair is a crown of withered white flowers. After a moment she slowly loosens and removes the rope from around her neck, adjusts her dirty white dress. She sways, humming.' This is Ophelia's song, paraphrased: and the image is inescapably associated with Shakespeare's maiden of shattered mind.

The weekly marches of Argentinian mothers around the Plaza de Mayo in Buenos Aires, when they silently cried for the thousands of disappeared sons and daughters, were called the marches of madwomen: *las locas de la Plaza de Mayo*. Gambaro's *Antigona Furiosa* had its origins there, in the fury and pain of the women deprived of their loved ones, in despair that could find consolation neither in a funeral rite nor a place for a grave. It is the daring spirit of *las locas* that feeds Gambaro's *Antigona*, which becomes an investigation through madness and from beyond death.

ANTIGONA'S BITTER VOICE

There are only two men propelling this vivisection of tragic events of the past: Coryphaeus and Antinous. They stay outside the cage that imprisons Antigona, passing the time in conversation, banter, and coffee. One can feel the slow pace of sleepy afternoons in a provincial Greek town where the men spend long hours . . . watching life around them like the action on a stage. There is an air of playful mockery in the tone of the men's dialogue, deliberately contrasted with the serious and bitter voice of Antigona:

> ANTINOUS: Why don't we celebrate?
> CORYPHAEUS (*darkly*): What is there to celebrate?
> ANTINOUS (*he lights up. Stupidly*): That peace has returned!
> CORYPHAEUS (*laughs*): I'll drink to that! Let's have a toast! What'll it be?
> ANTINOUS: Wine?
> CORYPHAEUS: Yes, lots of wine! And no coffee! (*Mimics Antigona.*) What is that dark liquid? Poison! (*Laughs, gasps hoarsely, faking a death rattle. After a moment, Antigona joins in. Antigona walks among her dead, in a strange gait in which she falls and recovers, falls and recovers.*)
> ANTIGONA: Corpses! Corpses! I walk on the dead. The dead surround me. Caress me . . . embrace me. . . . Ask me . . . what?

Coryphaeus and Antinous in Gambaro's play assume different roles but it is always Coryphaeus who, wearing 'Creon's shell'—torso, helmet, and arms—embodies the authority of a tyrant. Antinous appears as a jester and a collaborator with authority, who disguises his conformism with buoyancy.

Antigona, on the contrary, exhibits all her mournful passion without a distancing withdrawal. In the reconstructed scene of confrontation with Creon she cries and laments aloud: 'Do you see me, Creon? I am crying! Do you hear me, Creon?' There is a 'deep lament, raw and guttural'. Then she throws herself on the shroud as if discovering Polyneices' corpse: 'Oh, Polyneices, brother. Brother. Brother. I will be your breath. (*She pants as though she would revive him.*) Your mouth, your legs, your feet. I will cover you. I will cover you'. Several lines later Antigona cries to Polyneices: 'Brother, brother. I will be your body, your coffin, your earth! . . . The living are the great sepulchre of the dead! This is what Creon does not know! Nor his law!'

AN INDOMITABLE WOMAN

Antigona as envisioned by Griselda Gambaro is at once 'mad', as the Sophoclean heroine was—in her unyielding will, incomprehensible to others, and in her irrevocable decision to bury her brother in spite of the death penalty—yet also a sad, pitiable 'document in madness', as was Ophelia.

But the mind of Antigona Furiosa shines from time to time with vivid clarity and logic. Her capacity for grasping the events of the past and reflecting on them is demonstrated in several scenes—most forcefully in the re-enactment of Antigona's confrontation with Creon, but also in the scene of Creon and Haemon, and in the final scene of remembrance of her own death.

It is meaningful that in Gambaro's play it is Antigona who revivifies Haemon's voice. The motivation for this choice can be found in Sophocles' play, where Haemon is the only one who, as Creon puts it, has caught 'the very disease that grips her'.

> CORYPHAEUS (*as Creon*): That woman has gone to your head.
> ANTIGONA (*as Haemon*): I speak from the head, and not from the heart.
> CORYPHAEUS: In the voice of a woman . . . a perverse, indomitable woman.
> ANTIGONA: Perverse? Indomitable.

Haemon sees Antigona as 'indomitable', and she is the one who recreates his thoughts. Antigona in Gambaro's play slowly becomes indomitable through the broad range of human weakness. She does not conceal her emotions or her fear, dying at her own hand so as not to yield.

> ANTIGONA: I was afraid of hunger and thirst. Afraid I would weaken ignobly. At the last moment, crawl and beg.

In spite of her frailty, Antigona's will to bury Polyneices never weakens: 'I will always want to bury Polyneices. Though I a thousand times will live, and he a thousand times will die'. And in her final confession Gambaro's Antigona says: 'I didn't know I was born to share love, not hate. (*Long pause.*) But hate rules. (*Furious.*) The rest is silence!' And '*She kills herself, with fury*'.

When I was working as dramaturg for a production of Sophocles' *Antigone* in Europe, I remember an actress, struggling to perform the title-role, declaring: 'It's impossible; she is like a solid rock, formed before the play begins— she never really changes her mind; it is almost inhuman!' This actress had a very practical attitude to the role: she had to figure out how to present her character in the theatre of today. And she was right: Sophocles' Antigone presents a challenge for a contemporary actress because she is like a statue hewn in the hardest rock. Next to her, Gambaro's Antigona Furiosa looks malleable. But she, too, has the same invincible determination—not because of the gods, but because of her loved ones on this Earth.

NEVER LOSING A SENSE OF RIGHT AND WRONG

Janusz Glowacki brings up Antigone's name only once in his entire play—in its title. But although, at first glance, his drama does not utilize the actions or the characters of Sophocles' *Antigone,* the essence of the plot, with its sacrifice of the main character, Anita, is closely akin to ancient tragedy. Anita, a middle-aged Puerto Rican woman, is a homeless 'bag-lady' who lives in the bushes of Thompkins Square in New York. She might never have heard of the mythical Antigone, but she knows how Potter's Field was bought for Judas's silver.

In all her misery and confusion of mind, Anita is the only one who never loses a sense of right and wrong. When Paulie freezes to death in the park and is taken to Potter's Field, Anita comments: 'But why? That place is only for criminals and bums with no names and rejects. . . . It shouldn't be this way. It's wrong.' And later: 'A man who lies in a grave without his family is lonely forever'. When Sasha, her friend from the park, asks matter-of-factly, 'Did he have a family?' Anita answers, 'I am his family. (*Indicates the park.*) Here is his family'.

Glowacki's Anita rarely leaves her shopping cart off-guard: it is filled with all her belongings, with a pink telephone on the top. She is willingly, obsessively 'chained' to it, entrapped by this metal 'cage' in the same way as Gambaro's Antigona is 'caged' in a monstrous cell.

> ANITA: My mother died. I spent everything we saved to bury her in Puerto Rico. Then my brother stole the rest and went to prison and now I can't get back to Brooklyn because they won't let me on the subway with my cart so all my furniture is with the landlord.

There are two other men from the park who—along with the Policeman, who appears at intervals—function more as the ancient Chorus did, and as the male characters are utilized in Gambaro's play. Sasha and Flea have their own individual features, their obsessions with their past and hopes for the future: but the main focus of the plot is undeniably Anita-Antigone's.

LEVELS OF INSANITY

Anita not only looks (as one can read between Glowacki's lines) but also behaves as a person out of her wits or simply disturbed. All three of them—Sasha, Flea, Anita—seem to be disturbed: but it is Anita whose strange behaviour—hissing, 'casting evil's spell', rocking and musing to herself, pacing around the bench in circles, and above all burying their homeless comrade from the park—earns her the epithets 'crazy', 'mad', 'insane'.

That judgement is double-edged and has two meanings. She is considered mad in the same way the ancient Antigone was—fixed on a resolve beyond accepted rational thinking. But there is another level of insanity in Anita's case, which makes her act look blurry and deformed. This is the awkward, unpleasant air of a madwoman who believes that 'if you have a cashmere sweater it's best to get one with shoulder pads in it because that's where the bad luck collects'. Armed with such practical solutions, she embraces hope for a normal life: 'Now I have a phone so I can get work again, but I need a place to plug it in'.

Anita has invested all her savings—a sum that amounts to treasure in the life of the inhabitants of Thompkins Square

Park, nineteen dollars and fifty cents plus a pair of ski boots. She sends off a rescue party to recover Paulie's frozen body from the pile of coffins ready for shipment to Potter's Field. When the corpse of a bearded man arrives in the park, Sasha discovers their mistake in the daylight: it wasn't Paulie.

But Anita remains unaware. She prays and arranges an altar around the corpse seated on the bench. She and Sasha bury the dead man in a plastic bag behind the bench 'under the tree. He liked that tree.' While, in fear of the police, Anita and Sasha level the ground to conceal the traces of the grave, Anita remembers that Paulie did not recognize her after five years' absence in the park since the time he 'loved her'. 'I think he did recognize me. He only pretended not to. How can you not recognize the person you love?'

I find this reaffirmation of love in the absence of physical recognition of a loved one the essential and most valuable motif in Glowacki's drama. Glowacki deliberately dwells on it, making it surface and reappear again, the theme culminating when Paulie's buried body is not found, although the police dig up half of the park in their search. Then a fence is built around the park, and a serious scrutiny of its inhabitants is conducted.

The Policeman, who has the last speech in Glowacki's play, reports on its climactic events: 'The source of the gossip was a crazy Puerto Rican woman who used to live there. The woman kept trying to get back in even after we put up a ten foot high cyclone fence. Finally she hung herself off the main gate. She was taken to Potter's Field'.

All three plays based on the myth of Antigone—the ancient version by Sophocles, and these two modern variants—portray the greatness of human independence. In all three the audience shares the playwright's empathy for Antigone, and her madness, in whatever form, wins acceptance as morally valuable. However, in Sophocles' rendering of the myth, Antigone does not undergo the transformation which is crucial in these contemporary versions. In both plays we can observe an evolution of a main character who transcends poverty and obscurity to attain through moral revolt the stature of heroine. The Policeman in Glowacki's *Antigone in New York* comments on this phenomenon, remarking: 'Well, what can you do? Some people are beyond help'.

APPENDIX A

THE ORIGINS OF THEATER

The theater as people know it today—actors playing roles before an audience of spectators—was born in ancient Greece. Of that much scholars are sure. However, the exact origins of various theatrical conventions, or basic elements and practices, such as comedy, tragedy, and acting, remain shrouded in mystery. The Greeks, Egyptians, and other ancient peoples left very few written descriptions of themselves and their lives before the sixth century B.C. And of the primitive peoples that preceded them, all that we know is what scientists can deduce from studying bones, crude tools, and other decaying artifacts. So it is not surprising that frustrated scholars find the development of drama difficult to trace. "It is exasperating that the origin of something so significant should be so obscure," comments historian Lionel Casson. "No one knows for certain under what circumstances or precisely when the Greeks got the brilliant idea of having men impersonate imaginary characters."

STORIES TOLD THROUGH DANCE

Yet while the exact origins of drama may be obscure, it has been possible to make educated guesses about how people first began acting out certain events from their lives. Anthropologists (scientists who study human cultures) believe that early storytelling was one source of drama. According to this view, primitive hunters may have reenacted their hunting exploits for members of the family or tribe gathered around the campfire, as well as for their gods. In this context, the hunter would have taken on the role of actor and his listeners that of audience. Such early storytelling probably predated the development of complex language. So, anthropologists believe, initially it likely took the form of dance. As famed theatrical scholar Sheldon Cheney puts it:

> After the activities that secure to primitive peoples the material necessities, food and shelter, the dance comes first. It is the earliest outlet for emotion, and the beginning of the

arts. . . . Primitive man, poor in means of expression, with only the rudimentary beginnings of spoken language, universally expressed his deeper feelings through measured movement. . . . He danced for pleasure and as ritual. He spoke in dance to his gods, he prayed in dance and gave thanks in dance. By no means all this activity was dramatic or theatric; but in his designed movement was the germ of drama and of theater. . . . The noises man made, as he rhythmically moved, took on the measure of the swaying body and the tapping feet, gradually became war-song or prayer, developed into traditional tribal chant, [and] ultimately led to conscious poetry.

In most cultures the poetry of storytelling remained, for the most part, a part of religious ritual. Indeed, in Greece, as in other lands, formal dramatic poetry, along with music and dance, early became associated with religious ceremony. In particular, poetry was prominent in the rituals associated with the god Dionysus. In the early Greek myths, according to theater historian Oscar G. Brockett,

> Dionysus was the son of Zeus (the greatest of Greek gods). . . . Reared by satyrs [mythical creatures, half-man and half-goat] he was killed, dismembered, and resurrected. As a god he was associated with fertility, wine, and revelry, while the events of his life linked him with . . . the cycle of the seasons, and the recurring pattern of birth, maturity, death, and rebirth. Through their rites, Dionysian worshippers sought a mystical union with the primal [most primitive] creative urge. On a more practical level, they sought to promote fertility: to guarantee the return of spring . . . and ample harvests.

THE GOAT-SONG

Worship of Dionysus, along with that of the other Greek gods, developed between the fourteenth and eighth centuries B.C. Little is known about this formative period of the people now referred to as the classical Greeks, whose splendid literature and art of the fifth and fourth centuries B.C. so influenced later civilizations, including today's. What is certain is that by the eighth century B.C. Dionysian ritual had developed a kind of poetry and ceremony known as dithyramb. This special form of verse, sung and danced to by the worshipers, became the highlight of the religious festivals dedicated to the god. The dithyramb, which told the story of Dionysus or in some way honored him, widened over time to include other gods, as well as some human heroes. The dithyramb also took on an increasingly dramatic form in which a priest led a group of worshipers, called a chorus, in chanting and dancing before the rest of the congregation. No examples of this verse have survived. But the opening of *The Suppliants*, a play by the fifth-century-B.C. playwright Aeschylus (older books often use the spelling Aeschulus), probably captures the general form and atmosphere of the original dithyrambic procession. To the music of flutes and cymbals, a chorus of fifty maidens clad in white robes approaches an altar and rhythmically chants:

> Zeus! Lord and guard of suppliant hands!
> Look down benign [favorably] on us who crave
> Thine aid—whom winds and waters drave [drove]
> From where, through drifting shifting sands,
> Pours [the river] Nilus to the wave.

Certain men, at first probably priests, became adept at composing new versions of dithyramb. By creating material specifically to be performed before an audience, they may have been, in a sense, the first playwrights. This is certainly how Aristotle saw it. In his *Poetics*, written in the late fourth century B.C., he theorized that tragedy, the first definite form of drama, originated in Dionysian ritual. Tragedy, said Aristotle,

> certainly began in improvisations [spontaneous pieces] ... originating with the authors of the dithyramb ... which still survive ... in many of our cities. And its advance [as drama] after that was little by little, through their improving on whatever they had before them at each stage.

Supporters of this view point out that the dithyramb was also called "goat-song" because of the involvement of men dressed as satyrs in the ceremony. The term "tragedy," they say, probably developed from the Greek words *tragos*, meaning goat, and *odi*, meaning song.

THE SUSPENSE OF ANTICIPATION

Another source of drama in Greece was epic poetry. For centuries, wandering poets known as bards had recited the heroic deeds of gods and human heroes from Greece's dim past. Homer, a legendary bard possibly of the ninth or eighth century B.C., was credited with composing the two most famous epic poems, the *Iliad* and the *Odyssey*. The first took place in the final year of the Greeks' ten-year siege of the powerful kingdom of Troy to rescue Sparta's Queen Helen, who had been abducted by a Trojan prince. The other epic recounted the adventures of the Greek hero Odysseus (or Ulysses) on his way back from the siege.

At first, presentation of the epics was informal. A bard merely stood before a group of townspeople and recited the stories. In time, however, as Greek society became more organized and urbanized, such reciting was more formal. In the eighth and seventh centuries B.C., city-states became the main focus of Greek civilization. Each of these tiny independent nations consisted of a central town and its surrounding villages and farms. By the mid–sixth century, Athens, located on the Attic peninsula in eastern Greece, had become the largest and most influential of the city-states. It had also become the most cultured, with the government spending growing sums to promote the arts and public festivals. In about 566 B.C., seeking to enhance a popular festival, the Athenian leader Solon instituted the *rhapsodia*, contests in which various reciters delivered portions of the *Iliad* and *Odyssey* before a large crowd.

These formal dramatic recitations, like the dithyramb, became very popular with the Athenian populace. Audiences found both presentations exciting and moving, even though they already knew the plots and outcomes. As theater scholar Edmund Fuller explains:

> It is the peculiar power of drama that a play can be utterly gripping to its audience even when everyone knows perfectly well how it is going to end. Indeed, it often draws its greatest force from the fact that we *do* know what is coming. The suspense of anticipation is greater than that of surprise, for the real nature of suspense is anguish, concern for the characters because of our sympathy for them. What fascinates us is how they respond to what happens.

THE FIRST ACTOR

Later, around 534 B.C., Athens began holding a lavish annual festival known as the City Dionysia, in honor of Dionysus. Both formal dithyramb and *rhapsodia* were presented at this festival, which featured Athens's most popular dramatic contest yet. The first winner of this contest was a poet named Thespis, who developed the dramatic presentations into a new form called tragedy. This first version of what is now recognized as a theatrical play utilized most of the elements of the dithyramb and the *rhapsodia*, but added some important new ideas. Among the innovations of Thespis, for instance, was the addition of a chorus to the *rhapsodia*. The members of the chorus recited in unison some of the lines and also commented on the events of the story, to focus audience attention more on the passion, plight, and suffering of the heroes. Thespis's other novel idea was actually to impersonate, rather than just tell about, the story's heroes. Theater historian Phyllis Hartnoll states:

The great innovation that Thespis made was to detach himself from the chorus [of both dithyramb and *rhapsodia*] and, in the person of the god or hero whose deeds were celebrated, to engage in dialogue with it. He was thus the first actor as well as the first manager [producer-director]. The step he took was even more revolutionary than it seems to us, for he was the first unsanctified person [nonpriest] who dared to assume the character of a god.

In a sense, Thespis created the formal theater overnight. In utilizing dialogue between himself, the first actor, and the chorus, he introduced the basic convention of theatrical plays, namely, characters reciting set speeches, the content of which moves the story along. He also experimented with ways of disguising himself so that he could portray different characters in the same dramatic piece. He eventually decided on masks, which became another basic convention of Greek, and later Roman, theater. In addition, Thespis helped define the role of the audience. By enlarging the dithyramb into a piece of art and entertainment, he transformed the congregation into a true theater audience. For these innovations, Thespis became a theater immortal. As drama historian Marion Geisinger relates:

> The name of Thespis has come down to us in the use of the word *thespian* as a synonym for actor. Actually, the term seems originally to have referred to touring actors, because in ancient Greek vase paintings, Thespis is usually depicted seated on a cart; the tradition was that Thespis would take his actors [chorus members] around in this cart, which they used as a stage or performing platform. Whatever the reason, it seems most fitting to commemorate the first actor in the Western world by dubbing all those who have followed him with his name.

THE EARLY PLAYS

For subjects, Thespis and the playwrights who adopted his new form of entertainment and competed with him relied on the standard Greek myths, as well as on the tales in the *Iliad* and other epics now lost. They also depicted important recent historical events, especially attacks by the Persians on Greek cities in Asia Minor, what is now Turkey. Unfortunately, none of the plays of Thespis or his contemporaries have survived. Among these writer-actor-managers were Choerilus, who wrote some 160 plays and won the City Dionysia contest thirteen times, and Pratinas, who supposedly wrote 18 tragedies. Phrynichus, another popular writer, first won the contest sometime around 510 B.C. His most famous play was *The Fall of Miletus*, about the Persian take-over of the most prosperous Greek city in Asia Minor. According to the Greek historian Herodotus, this play was so moving that the audience burst into tears and city officials fined Phrynichus one thousand drachmas, a large sum of money at the time, for upsetting the citizenry.

Although the plays by Phrynichus, Choerilus, and Pratinas are lost, scattered fragments of these works and a few descriptions of them by later writers provide a rough idea of what the performances were like. Scholar James H. Butler, in *The Theater and Drama of Greece and Rome*, fills in some gaps:

> In performance, early Greek tragedies consisted of a series of acted episodes performed by one ... actor who also conversed with the leader of a chorus. During this action, chorus members reacted in patterned movements and gestures to what was happening.... Between episodes the chorus danced, recited in recitative [spoken words with musical accompaniment], and sang choral odes [songs] that related to past events or foreshadowed what was about to happen.

As such performances became increasingly elaborate and dramatic, the City Dionysia festival developed into a major holiday attraction, eagerly awaited each year by the populace. Covering several days at the end of March, the festival was open to all Greeks. The Athenian government wisely took the opportunity to use the celebration as a showcase of Athens's wealth and cultural achievements. To this end, the state financed the theater building and its maintenance, paid fees to the actors, and possibly the playwrights, and also provided prizes for the dramatic contests. All the other expenses of play production were the responsibility of the *choregi*, well-to-do Athenians asked by the state to help with the festival. These citizens were chosen by lot each year, and each *choregus* was assigned to a specific playwright. As Marion Geisinger explains:

> The *choregus* paid for the costumes, the sets, the training of the chorus, whatever supers (non-speaking extra roles) were required by the script, and the musicians. Obviously, the assignment of a generous *choregus* was an advantage to a playwright; that of a niggardly [cheap] one, a disadvantage.... Unhappy playwrights often felt that their failure to win the competition at the festival was the result of their being unable to mount their works properly, owing to the assignment of a stingy *choregus*.

The playwrights themselves also had weighty duties. In addition to writing plays, they acted in them, trained the chorus, composed the music, staged the dances, and supervised all other aspects of production. In fact, they were so involved in instructing others that at the time they were known as *didaskali*, or teachers.

Oscar Night in Athens

The playwrights rehearsed their works for months, right up until the beginning of the festival. On the first day, they, their *choregi* and chorus members, along with important public officials, took part in a stately and majestic procession. This colorful parade wound its way through the city and ended at the Theater of Dionysus, at the foot of the Acropolis, the stony hill on which the city's main temples and public buildings rested. After the public sacrifice of a bull to Dionysus, the dramatic competitions began. First came the dithyrambic contests. Then, over the course of the next few days, each of three playwrights presented three tragedies. In the late sixth century B.C., tragedy was still the main dramatic form, as comedy was not yet well developed or popular. When comedies eventually began to be performed at the City Dionysia in 501 B.C., they took place at night, after day-long presentations of tragedy.

The most eagerly awaited moment of the festival was the awards ceremony, in many ways an ancient counterpart of today's Oscar night. Lionel Casson states:

> A panel of ten judges issued four lists containing, respectively, the order in which they rated the tragic playwrights, comic playwrights, tragic leading actors, and comic leading actors. The victors—and that meant those who topped the lists; only first place really counted—were crowned with ivy, and the *choregi* hurried off to arrange farewell banquets for their casts.

As popular and exciting as these early festivals were, they were merely a prelude to what was to come. In the fifth century B.C. Athens produced a brief but magnificent burst of cultural activity, the brilliant results of which would thrill and awe the world ever after. Among the city's artists were a handful of gifted playwrights, among them Aeschylus, Sophocles, Euripides, and Aristophanes, who would in a stroke create the model for great theater for all times.

Appendix B

Greek Theatrical Production

As their early theaters and dramatic presentations evolved, the Greeks developed most of the aspects and conventions of play production that became standard through the ages. Among these were the use of scenery, costumes and disguises, chorus, dancing, and music, as well as acting styles and special visual and sound effects. The Greeks also built the first permanent theaters, some of which are still in use. All the theaters in later Western societies, from Rome to the present day, have employed variations of the basic physical layout devised by the Greeks.

We will never know exactly how the Greeks used these theatrical conventions and how their plays appeared on stage. The last authentic Greek productions were presented more than two thousand years ago. And later cultures, beginning with the Romans, modified the original Greek stagecraft to suit their own situations and tastes. Yet modern scholars have carefully studied drawings on Greek vases, many of which depict actors in costume and other theater scenes. They have also sifted through literary descriptions by Greek writers and archaeological evidence from the sites of ancient theaters. Using these clues, scholars have been able to piece together what should be a reasonably accurate picture of how Greek productions were staged.

The World's First Theater

The earliest versions of what eventually developed into theaters for play production were staging areas for religious ceremonies and celebrations. The first known example, and probably the oldest theater in the world, is in the palace at Knossus in northern Crete, the large island located southeast of the Greek mainland. This magnificent building was once the center of the main city in the empire of the Minoans, a non-Greek-speaking people who inhabited Crete and many other Greek islands between 2200 and 1450 B.C. By the time of the classical Greeks, Minoan civilization had long since vanished. Yet Minoan persons and events became key elements in classical Greek mythology. And many classical Greek cultural and religious practices had their roots in Minoan times.

The theatrical area at Knossus gives evidence of one such religious practice—the use of formal dancing and singing to honor the gods. In this area, stately and colorful religious rites, very likely similar to the later dithyramb, took place. The area consists of a rectangular court, roughly forty by thirty-five feet in size and paved with large irregular stones. The court is bordered on the east and south by steps on which, scholars believe, the spectators stood and sat. Greek archaeologist Anna Michailidou gives us this description:

> At the south-east corner of the Theater, in the angle between the two banks of steps, there is a bastion-like structure which is believed to have been a sort of royal box for the king and his family. We can imagine the monarch sitting there, surrounded by as many as 500 members of his court standing on the low steps, and watching the ... dances or religious rites.

The influence of the theatrical area at Knossus and similar areas at other Minoan palaces on later Greek theater design remains unclear. But it is likely that the basic concept of such ritual staging areas survived and became incorporated into the dithyramb in classical times. As the dithyramb evolved into formal theater in the sixth century B.C., the Greeks enlarged and modified these areas to accommodate play production.

CLASSICAL GREEK THEATERS

The first formal Greek theater was built in Athens between 550 and 534 B.C. Its exact location and physical layout are unknown, since the Athenians built over the site when larger theaters came into use a few years later. However, some evidence suggests that the first theater consisted of the same basic elements found in the Minoan versions, although considerably expanded. The rectangular court became the circular orchestra, or "dancing place," where the actors and chorus, as well as members of the dithyrambic processions, performed. And replacing the king's box was a central *thymele*, an altar for sacrificing to and honoring the gods. Surrounding much of the orchestra were wooden bleachers for the audience. The later Greek encyclopedia, the *Suidas*, reported that the bleachers collapsed in the middle of a performance, killing several spectators, about the year 499 B.C.

After this unfortunate incident, the Athenians built the Theater of Dionysus against the southeast base of the Acropolis. In its initial form, the theater had an orchestra some eighty-five feet in diameter with a *thymele* in the center. To avoid another disaster, the seating consisted of wooden planking covering earthen tiers carved into the hillside. In a later renovation, the wooden seats were replaced by the stone versions that have endured to the present. This audience area, which could accommodate more than fourteen thousand people, became known as the *theatron*, from which the word *theater* comes. On either side of the semi-circular *theatron* were the *parodoi*, entrances into the orchestra area used by actors and the chorus.

Early in the fifth century B.C. the theater's designers added a structure called the *skene* in front of and facing the orchestra and *theatron*. The word *skene* originally meant "scene building" and is the source of the word *scene* so often used today in stage and film presentations. The original scene building, according to scholar James T. Allen,

> served in the first instance as a background for the actors and provided accommodations for dressing-rooms and perhaps also for the storing of various properties [stage props]. It was of a rectangular shape, sometimes with projecting wings known as *paraskenia*...at the sides...and it was seldom, if ever, more than two stories in height. Originally constructed of wood or of other perishable materials the scene-building was at first temporary in character; apparently not until the fourth century was a *skene* of stone erected.

Later, other theaters copying the Dionysus arena's design appeared across Greece. The most beautiful and best preserved is the Theater of Epidauros, located about 110 miles southwest of Athens. Built around 350 B.C. by the architect Polyclitus the Younger, the stone structure is 387 feet across; it has a top seating tier 74 feet above orchestra level and a seating capacity of fourteen thousand. The Epidauros theater remains in such good condition that the Greek National Theater and other modern dramatic companies still perform in it.

THE PERFORMERS

It was through the *parodoi* in theaters like those of Dionysus and Epidauros that the choruses marched in the opening scenes of the ancient plays. As James Butler explains:

> The usual tragic and comic choruses entered singing the *parodos* (entrance song) and led by a flute player. They were grouped in a rectangular marching formation composed of

ranks and files—three by five for tragedy and four by six for comedy. Once in position in the orchestra, they turned and faced the spectators, still singing and gesturing.

During the performance that followed, the chorus members broke formation, moved from place to place, and reacted to the play's events and characters with appropriate verses and gestures. The chorus remained within the orchestra area until the finale, at which time it filed out, once more in formation and singing.

The chorus served several functions. First, it interacted with the actors, giving advice, asking questions, and expressing opinions. In Aeschylus's *The Persians,* for example, the chorus asks Persia's King Xerxes, whose armies the Greeks have defeated, "Is all your glory lost?" The king answers, "See you these poor remains of my torn robes?" "I see, I see," the chorus responds. Also, the chorus's singing and movements, which could be happy and animated or somber and morose, set the overall mood of the play and heightened the dramatic effect. In addition, says Oscar Brockett, the chorus served "an important rhythmical function, creating pauses or retardations [slowing down the action] during which the audience [could] reflect upon what had happened and what was to come."

The actors who interacted with the chorus wore elaborate masks that covered the whole head, resting on the shoulders. Made of linen stiffened with clay and brightly painted, each mask represented a stock character, such as a young maiden, a middle-aged man, an evil king, or a certain god. Writing in the second century A.D., the Greek scholar Julius Pollux listed and described many standard Greek theatrical masks. For example, for tragedy there were six for old men, eight for young men, three for male servants, and eleven for various women; for comedy, nine for older men, eleven for younger men, seven for male servants, and seventeen for women. Special masks for gods, as well as for satyrs and other mythical creatures, were also used. Comments scholar Bernard M.W. Knox:

> The masks certainly ruled out the play of facial expression which we regard today as one of the actor's most important skills, but in the Theater of Dionysus, where even the front row of spectators was sixty feet away from the stage (the back rows were three hundred feet away), facial expression could not have been seen anyway. And the masks had a practical value. They made it possible for the same actor to play two or even three or four different parts in different scenes of the play.

The masks also made it possible for men to play women's roles, an important and closely observed convention in ancient Greek theater. Apparently the Greeks considered it improper for women to bare their emotions, even staged ones, in public.

While the masks may have prevented the actors from utilizing facial expressions, they did not limit the use of voices. According to Oscar Brockett:

> The Greeks seem to have placed considerable emphasis upon the voice, for they judged actors above all by beauty of vocal tone and ability to adapt manner of speaking to mood and character.... The plays demanded three kinds of delivery: speech, recitative, and song. As the primary means of expression, the voice was trained and exercised by the actor much as it might be by an opera singer today. While the best actors attained high standards of vocal excellence, others apparently ranted and roared.

COSTUMES, PROPS, AND SCENERY

Like the masks, Greek theatrical costumes were brightly colored. This was partly to catch the eye from a distance, since most of the spectators sat so far from the actors. Another function of the bright colors was to aid in character recognition. Women's gowns, for instance, were usually of a particular color. A queen's costume was almost always purple, the traditional color of royalty, so that the spectators, who had no programs, could instantly recognize the character. Costume color also denoted mood. A character in mourning or undergoing extreme misfortune, for example, would wear black. In general, says theater historian H.C. Baldry, the actor's "own physical identity was completely concealed: mask, costume and footwear together covered him entirely except for his hands. His robe was usually ankle-length."

The actors also used props, as they do today, although the Greeks tended to use them sparingly. The most common examples were chariots, statues of gods, couches, shields and swords, and biers on which dead bodies were displayed. Special props were also associated with specific characters. Marion Geisinger states:

> To differentiate among the gods and the heroes, certain easily recognizable properties were carried. Apollo [the sun god] carried his bow, Hermes [god of invention] his magic wand, Hercules [a heroic strongman] carried his club and lion skin, and Perseus [a clever hero] his cap of darkness. Warriors usually appeared in full armor, with a short scarlet cloak draped around the arm. An old man would carry a staff; a messenger

of good tidings wore a crown of olives or of laurel. A king would carry a spear and wear a crown.

While costumes and props tended to be fairly realistic, Greek theatrical producers left the settings largely to the audience's imagination. This was partly because the design of the open-air theaters placed a strict limitation on the kinds of setting a playwright could depict. In classical times, as a rule, the action of the plays took place outdoors, in front of a house, palace, temple, or other familiar structure. Once added to theaters, the fixed *skene*, redecorated appropriately by the producer, represented the fronts of these buildings. Interiors could not be shown, and there is no solid evidence for the existence in early Greek theaters of movable painted scenery like that used today. However, according to tradition, Sophocles introduced the idea of painting descriptive backgrounds on the immovable *skene*, a practice that subsequently became common.

SPECIAL EFFECTS

Partly to overcome the inability to show interiors, in the late fifth century B.C. the Greeks introduced the *eccyclema*, or "tableau machine." Violent acts such as murders were almost always committed "indoors," and therefore offstage and out of sight, and the audience learned about them secondhand from messengers and other characters. Sometimes, however, to achieve shock value, a doorway in the *skene* would open and stagehands would push out the *eccyclema*, a movable platform on rollers. On the platform, frozen in a posed and dramatic tableau, would be usually both murderer and victim. In the climax of productions of Aeschylus's play *Agamemnon*, for example, an *eccyclema* probably displayed the body of the slain king. Standing over Agamemnon's corpse was his wife and killer, Clytemnestra, weapon in hand. Despite knowing full well this scene was coming, the spectators usually gasped in horror.

The Greeks developed special theatrical effects of other kinds to heighten the stage spectacle. Julius Pollux described a *keraunoskopeion*, or "lightning machine," and a *bronteion*, or "thunder machine," but unfortunately he did not explain how these devices worked. Perhaps the most spectacular engine of special effects was the *machina*, from which the word *machine* is derived. As Eugene O'Neill Jr. explains, "Frequently at the close of a play the dramatist introduced a god into the action, who would naturally be expected to appear from above. He apparently was brought in by some kind of crane or derrick, called the 'machine.'" This mechanical arm probably was raised by ropes and pulleys, and the actor playing the god dangled from it on a hook.

The *machina* was also used to show spectacular human exploits, such as the hero Bellerophon riding the flying horse Pegasus. Comedy writers and producers used the *machina* in a humorous way. In Aristophanes' play *Peace*, for instance, a nonheroic farmer flew a giant dung beetle over the orchestra and *skene* and shouted, "Hi, crane-operator, take care of me!" Invariably, though, most playwrights used the device to fly in gods for the finale, an approach that eventually became overused. O'Neill comments, "The term *deus ex machina*, 'the god from the machine,' has become standard in dramatic criticism. It . . . refers to awkward, mechanical, and unconvincing means which a playwright is forced to employ if he cannot work out a satisfactory resolution to his plot."

CAUGHT UP IN THE EXCITEMENT

All these theatrical elements—masks, costumes, machines, and the like—were designed to entertain the audience. The playwrights and producers demonstrably attained this goal, for the theater was immensely popular in Greece. In Athens in the fifth century B.C., for example, performances were always sold out. The Athenians, it seems, also invented the theater ticket. This was necessary because nearly all the city's two hundred thousand or more people desired entrance into a building that seated no more than seventeen thousand at its largest expansion. Yet playgoing was not exclusively a pastime of the well-to-do. About the year 450 B.C., the democratic leader Pericles instituted a special government fund to provide tickets for the poor.

Greek theater audiences differed from modern ones mainly in their outward show of enthusiasm. As James H. Butler puts it:

> If it were possible to project ourselves back in time, to attend a series of performances at one of the great festivals given in the Theater of Dionysus, the strongest impressions we would have, aside from those caused by strange scenic and acting conventions, would be of the audience. For they were caught up in a feverish excitement, an intense interest in the outcome of the various contests. Their volatility and enthusiasm were more characteristic of present-day football and baseball

spectators than of the quiet . . . often passive demeanor exhibited by our theater audiences. The hundreds directly competing for prizes and honors in the City Dionysia sharpened the appetite for victory. Add to this group several hundred, perhaps several thousand, former chorus members, dithyrambic performers, flute players, and extras sprinkled among the audience. They had competed in previous festivals and were quite knowledgeable on the finer points and techniques of performance. Refreshments to sustain the "dawn to dusk" audience were hawked [sold by roving vendors], thereby increasing the general noise and commotion.

Greek audiences differed from today's in another way. Because the Greeks invented the theater, their audiences witnessed something unique, an institution that existed nowhere else and developed and evolved before their eyes. Theatrical conventions and ideas that today seem run-of-the-mill were, in ancient Athens, fresh and exciting. It was in this stimulating, creative atmosphere that some of the greatest playwrights of all time, including Sophocles, worked their magic.

CHRONOLOGY

B.C.

CA. 496

Sophocles is born at Colonus, near Athens.

468

Sophocles wins his first top prize at the great City Dionysia dramatic festival for the play *Triptolemus,* beating Aeschylus, the greatest dramatist of the time.

CA. 447

Sophocles writes and produces *Ajax.*

443

The great Athenian statesman Pericles appoints Sophocles treasurer of the federated city-states making up Athens's empire.

CA. 442–441

Sophocles writes and produces *Antigone.*

440

Sophocles is elected one of Athens's ten generals, supposedly largely due to the popularity of *Antigone.*

CA. 429

Sophocles writes and produces *Oedipus the King,* which later generations will judge his masterpiece.

406

Sophocles writes *Oedipus at Colonus,* the sequel to *Oedipus the King* and prequel to *Antigone;* Sophocles dies, supposedly while reciting odes from *Antigone.*

405

Tributes to Sophocles appear in the lines of the comic play *Frogs,* by his colleague Aristophanes.

CA. 335–322

The Greek philosopher/scholar Aristotle writes the *Poetics*, in which he praises Sophocles' writing skill.

330

To discourage corruption of the original text, the Athenian statesman Lycurgus establishes an official version of *Antigone.*

A.D.

1502

The first printed version of *Antigone* appears.

1770–1831

Life of the German philosopher Georg W.F. Hegel, whose detailed commentary on *Antigone* will exert considerable influence on later scholars.

1845

The first professional American stage production of *Antigone* opens in New York City.

1913

Famed psychoanalyst Sigmund Freud publishes *Totem and Taboo,* in which he details the "Oedipus complex," a theory of human sexual desires based on the relationships in Sophocles' *Oedipus the King.*

1944

Noted classical scholar C.M. Bowra publishes his highly acclaimed study of Sophocles' works, *Sophoclean Tragedy;* French playwright Jean Anouilh writes and produces a modern version of Sophocles' *Antigone.*

1947

Another modern version of *Antigone,* this one by German playwright Bertolt Brecht, is first staged.

1982

A widely regarded new English translation of *Antigone* by Robert Fagles appears.

1993

San Francisco's American Conservatory Theater receives favorable notices for its production of Sophocles' *Antigone;* playwright Janusz Glowacki's modern version of the play, *Antigone in New York,* premieres in Washington, D.C.

FOR FURTHER RESEARCH

ABOUT SOPHOCLES AND HIS WORKS

Aristotle, *Poetics*. In Robert Maynard Hutchins, ed., *The Works of Aristotle*, in *Great Books of the Western World Series*. Chicago: Encyclopaedia Britannica, 1952. Contains the philosopher's famous critique of Greek literature, including Sophocles' *Antigone* and *Oedipus the King*.

William N. Bates, *Sophocles: Poet and Dramatist*. New York: Russell and Russell, 1969.

C.M. Bowra, *Sophoclean Tragedy*. Oxford: Clarendon Press, 1944.

Michael Grant, *The Classical Greeks*. New York: Charles Scribner's Sons, 1989. Contains a biographical sketch of Sophocles and his works.

G.M. Kirkwood, *A Study of Sophoclean Drama*. Ithaca, NY: Cornell University Press, 1958.

Bernard M.W. Knox, *The Heroic Temper: Studies in Sophoclean Tragedy*. Berkeley and Los Angeles: University of California Press, 1966.

Don Nardo, ed., *Readings on Sophocles*. San Diego: Greenhaven Press, 1997.

David Seale, *Vision and Stagecraft in Sophocles*. Chicago: University of Chicago Press, 1982.

Cedric H. Whitman, *Sophocles: A Study of Heroic Humanism*. Cambridge, MA: Harvard University Press, 1951.

Thomas Woodward, ed., *Sophocles: A Collection of Critical Essays*. Englewood Cliffs, NJ: Prentice-Hall, 1966.

TRANSLATIONS AND STUDIES OF *ANTIGONE*

Richard E. Braun, trans., *Sophocles:* Antigone. New York: Oxford University Press, 1973.

Robert Fagles, trans., *Sophocles: The Three Theban Plays: Antigone, Oedipus the King, Oedipus at Colonus.* New York: Penguin Books, 1984.

Dudley Fitts and Robert Fitzgerald, trans., *Sophocles: The Oedipus Cycle* (Antigone, Oedipus the King, Oedipus at Colonus). New York: Harcourt, Brace and World, 1969.

Robert F. Goheen, *The Imagery of Sophocles'* Antigone: *A Study of Poetic Language and Structure.* Princeton, NJ: Princeton University Press, 1951.

David Grene, trans., *Antigone.* In David Grene and Richmond Lattimore, eds., *Greek Tragedy.* Vol. 1. Chicago: University of Chicago Press, 1991.

H.D.F. Kitto, trans., Edith Hall, ed., *Sophocles:* Antigone, Oedipus the King, Electra. New York: Oxford University Press, 1994.

William A. Landes, ed., *Antigone.* Studio City, CA: Players' Press, 1995.

Joan V. O'Brien, *Guide to Sophocles'* Antigone. Carbondale: Southern Illinois University Press, 1978.

Nicholas Rudall, trans., *Antigone.* Chicago: Ivan R. Dee, 1998.

TRANSLATIONS OF OTHER PLAYS BY SOPHOCLES

Richard C. Jebb, trans., *The Complete Plays of Sophocles.* New York: Bantam Books, 1967.

Bernard M.W. Knox, trans., *Oedipus the King.* New York: Pocket Books, 1959.

John Moore, trans., *Ajax.* In David Grene and Richmond Lattimore, eds., *Sophocles.* Vol. 2. Chicago: University of Chicago Press, 1957.

F. Storr, trans., *Sophocles: Complete Works.* 2 vols. Cambridge, MA: Harvard University Press, 1967.

Charles R. Walker, trans., *Oedipus the King and Oedipus at Colonus.* New York: Doubleday, 1966.

E.F. Watling, trans., *Sophocles: Electra and Other Plays.* Baltimore: Penguin Books, 1953.

ANCIENT GREEK DRAMA, THEATER, AND LITERATURE

James T. Allen, *Stage Antiquities of the Greeks and Romans and Their Influence.* New York: Cooper Square, 1963.

H.C. Baldry, *The Greek Tragic Theater.* New York: W.W. Norton, 1971.

James H. Butler, *The Theater and Drama of Greece and Rome.* San Francisco: Chandler, 1972.

Lionel Casson, *Masters of Ancient Comedy.* New York: Macmillan, 1960.

John Ferguson, *A Companion to Greek Tragedy.* Austin: University of Texas Press, 1972.

Moses Hadas, ed., *The Complete Plays of Aristophanes.* New York: Bantam Books, 1962.

Karelisa V. Hartigan, *Greek Tragedy on the American Stage: Ancient Drama in the Commercial Theater, 1882–1994.* Westport, CT: Greenwood Press, 1995.

H.D.F. Kitto, *Greek Tragedy.* Garden City, NY: Doubleday, 1952.

———, *Form and Meaning in Drama: A Study of Six Greek Plays and of* Hamlet. London: Methuen, 1956.

Peter Levi, *A History of Greek Literature.* New York: Penguin Books, 1985.

D.W. Lucas, *The Greek Tragic Poets.* New York: W.W. Norton, 1959.

Gilbert Murray, *The Literature of Ancient Greece.* Chicago: University of Chicago Press, 1956.

Don Nardo, *Greek and Roman Theater.* San Diego: Lucent Books, 1995.

Gilbert Norwood, *Greek Tragedy.* New York: Hill and Wang, 1960.

Arthur Pickard-Cambridge, *The Dramatic Festivals of Athens.* Oxford: Oxford University Press, 1968.

C.A. Robinson, ed., *An Anthology of Greek Drama.* New York: Holt, Rinehart, and Winston, 1960.

Paul Roche, trans., *The Orestes Plays of Aeschylus.* New York: New American Library, 1962.

ANCIENT GREEK SOCIETY AND CULTURE

Lesley Adkins and Roy A. Adkins, *Handbook to Life in Ancient Greece.* New York: Facts On File, 1997.

Sue Blundell, *Women in Ancient Greece.* Cambridge, MA: Harvard University Press, 1995.

C.M. Bowra, *The Greek Experience.* New York: New American Library, 1957.

E.R. Dodds, *The Greeks and the Irrational.* Berkeley and Los Angeles: University of California Press, 1951.

Michael Grant, *Myths of the Greeks and Romans.* New York: New American Library, 1962.

Edith Hamilton, *The Greek Way to Western Civilization.* New York: New American Library, 1942.

Victor D. Hanson, *The Western Way of War: Infantry Battle in Classical Greece.* New York: Oxford University Press, 1989.

Victor D. Hanson and John Heath, *Who Killed Homer? The Demise of Classical Education and the Recovery of Greek Wisdom.* New York: Free Press, 1998.

Joint Association of Classical Teachers, *The World of Athens: An Introduction to Classical Athenian Culture.* New York: Cambridge University Press, 1984.

Robert B. Kebric, *Greek People.* Mountain View, CA: Mayfield, 1997.

Thomas R. Martin, *Ancient Greece: From Prehistoric to Hellenistic Times.* New Haven, CT: Yale University Press, 1996.

Don Nardo, *The Age of Pericles.* San Diego: Lucent Books, 1996.

———, *The Trial of Socrates.* San Diego: Lucent Books, 1997.

———, *Greek and Roman Science.* San Diego: Lucent Books, 1997.

———, *The Parthenon.* San Diego: Lucent Books, 1999.

———, *Greek and Roman Sports.* San Diego: Lucent Books, 1999.

———, *Life in Ancient Athens.* San Diego: Lucent Books, 2000.

Robert Payne, *Ancient Greece: The Triumph of a Culture.* New York: W.W. Norton, 1964.

Sarah B. Pomeroy, *Goddesses, Whores, Wives, and Slaves: Women in Classical Antiquity.* New York: Shocken Books, 1995.

Ian Scott-Kilvert, trans., *The Rise and Fall of Athens: Nine Greek Lives by Plutarch.* New York: Penguin Books, 1960.

Nigel Spivey, *Greek Art.* London: Phaidon Press, 1997.

Alfred Zimmern, *The Greek Commonwealth.* New York: Modern Library, 1931.

INDEX